BIRMINGHA THE WAR YEARS

Alton & Jo Douglas

King George VI, with the Town Hall as a backcloth, inspects the Guard of Honour, as part of his "Thank You" tour, 7th November 1945.

© Alton and Jo Douglas 1995
ISBN 1 85858 100 1
Published by Brewin Books, Doric House, 56 Alcester Road, Studley, Warwickshire B80 7LG.

Printed by Warwick Printing Co. Ltd., Theatre Street, Warwick CV34 4DR.

Layout by Alton and Jo Douglas
All Rights Reserved
4th Impression – April 2002

Birmingham Co-operative Society Ltd., Transport Dept. Fire Service, Great Brook Street, Nechells, 1940.

FRONT COVER: The Duke of Gloucester takes the salute, as the Home Guard march past, 14th January 1943.

Contents

Dear Nostalgic,

Welcome to the safe pages of a book that covers Birmingham's most dramatic and dangerous years. Over half-a-century ago, our fellow-citizens faced up to an enemy, on their own doorsteps, with that indomitable British spirit, which seems to be a mixture of "Do your worst - see if I care" and "A funny thing happened on the way to the air-raid shelter". We wish to pay tribute to that wartime spirit without in any way glorifying war itself, always remembering that, for a great many people, Birmingham was the Front Line.

To avoid repetition, we have not included much in the way of facts and figures as so much detail was given in our previous books, Birmingham at War Vols 1 and 2. This time, in date order (or as near as memory will allow) we are presenting a scrapbook of events, with lots and lots of local happenings and, here and there, an impression of how the war was developing on the wider scale.

The one lesson we have learned, since those early books, is that you prefer to look at the items in our publications and pour out your own stories - but I can't resist one anecdote, just to set you talking!

After I had spoken at a dinner in Sidmouth a man came up to me and, in an unmistakeable German accent said, "I would like to purchase one of your war books". I gulped and replied, "I don't think you'll like the final outcome". He patted me on the shoulder and said, "Don't worry, I was born in Smethwick".

Thank you to everyone who helped with this book and, in particular, our friend Dennis Moore, who always seems to know the answer before we've asked the question. By the way, Dennis began the war as a schoolboy picking up hot shrapnel in the street and finished it flying in bombing raids over Germany.

So, whether you were fighting in foreign parts or here, in our own city, this book comes with the gratitude of all of us.

Yours, in friendship,

Alton

The Territorial Army marches past the General Hospital, as they return from camp at Winchcombe, 15th August 1937.

PROLOGUE

There are those who consider that the Second World War became a certainty with the signing of the Treaty of Versailles on 28th June 1919. Ratified on 10th January 1920, it framed the setting up of The League of Nations. Certain German territories were to be surrendered to France and Poland; Germany was forbidden to possess submarines or maintain any military or naval air-force (the German naval fleet already having been surrendered except for a few light units). Reparations, the term used for the compensation for damage done to property by the German armies in the Great War, as it was then known, were punitive and this did nothing to contain Germany's anger and despondency in defeat.

In the event, Germany, under Adolph Hitler, who had become Reich Chancellor in 1933, made secret moves to raise a substantial army and air-force and built pocket-battleships which remained within internationally-agreed tonnage limits.

Germany re-occupied the Rhineland in 1936 and Austria and Czechoslovakia were annexed in 1938 and 1939. Hitler's war machine was almost ready for action but Britain's Prime Minister (and Birmingham's son) Neville Chamberlain, was in Munich to sign the famous (or infamous) agreement with Hitler on 29th September 1938. Hitler was appeased and no doubt considered Britain a soft touch. He denounced the Polish Non-Aggression Treaty on 28th April 1939. Britain countered in May by signing the Anglo-Polish Treaty, pledging to go to the aid of Poland if she were attacked. Some three months later German troops invaded Poland on 1st September 1939. Britain was committed and at 11am, 3rd September, Neville Chamberlain's sombre and moving tones told us on the wireless that a state of war existed between Britain and Germany. We called it "Hitler's War", then later "The Second World War" and when America entered the fray, "World War II".

The Lord Mayor, Alderman Samuel Grey, gets to grips with an anti-aircraft gun, Council House, 14th July 1936.

Sound locaters practising, 199th Battery, 69th Royal Warks. Regt., Anti-Aircraft Brigade, Royal Artillery (T.A.) General Electric Co. Ltd., Witton, 1937.

Searchlight instruction for the Territorials, Kingstanding Road, 1937.

AIR RAID WARDENS SERVICE IN BIRMINGHAM

REGIONAL INSPECTOR AT HARBORNE

The part that women can play in the air raid precautions scheme was explained by Commander Donald C. Morrison, Regional Inspector of the Home Office Air Raid Precautions Department, to an audience of men and women at Station Road Council Schools, Harborne, last night. In Birmingham, he said, 1,100 volunteers had enrolled as air raid wardens, and of these 200 were women. The authorities were very anxious to get a large number of women to assist in the various services, and particularly in dealing with incendiary bombs. Various experiments in which women had taken part after a very short training showed that they could deal effectively with incendiary bombs.

Speaking of the organisation of the service, Commander Morrison said the Home Office recommended that posts to which two or three wardens would be attached should be established in sectors including about five hundred inhabitants. They required for wardens men and women who were steady-minded, unafraid and with a good share of common sense. Probably their worst job would be to prevent panic. They must get to know their neighbours, and must certainly know every inch of their sector. In time of emergency they would have to advise their neighbours as to how to make their rooms gas-proof. They would probably also assist in the distribution of gas masks to people in their sector, and it would be as well if they tried to make a census with a view to ascertaining the sizes of respirators that would be necessary. 21.12.37

The colours of the 190th and 191st Batteries, 69th Royal Warks. Regt., Anti-Aircraft Brigade, Royal Artillery (T.A.) are carried into Christ Church, Burney Lane, Stechford, at the start of a recruiting week, 24th April 1938.

The Duke of Gloucester reviews the troops, Victoria Square,15th July 1938.

The Prime Minister, Neville Chamberlain, meets Hitler for the second time, 22nd September 1938.

We, the German Führer and Chancellor and the British Prime Minister, have had a further meeting today and are agreed in recognising that the question of Anglo-German relations is of the first importance for the two countries and for Europe.

We regard the agreement signed last night and the Anglo-German Naval Agreement as symbolic of the desire of our two peoples never to go to war with one another again.

We are resolved that the method of consultation shall be the method adopted to deal with any other questions that may concern our two countries, and we are determined to continue our efforts to remove possible sources of difference and thus to contribute to assure the peace of Europe.

The "scrap of paper" that Chamberlain brought back with him, signed by both men.

King George VI (on right) and Queen Elizabeth visit the Austin Motor Company on the occasion of the first Fairey Battle aircraft being produced, March 1939.

Join the unit your pals are joining—

THE DUNLOP UNIT of the TERRITORIALS

The first recruit of the day to sign up, at the T.A. Information Bureau, is congratulated by the Lord Mayor, Alderman James Crump, Council House, 21st April 1939.

Warks. Yeomanry Despatch Riders, Ragley Hall, Alcester, May 1939.

Warks. Yeomanry set up camp, 20th May 1939.

Signing up for the forthcoming conflict, James Watt Street Recruiting Office, 25th August 1939. Two days before war was declared the War Office called up all Reservists and Territorials and they were absorbed into the Regular Army.

Teachers Called Back By Radio

TEACHERS in evacuation areas throughout the country were notified in a Ministry of Health notice broadcast at 9.45 last night "that it is considered desirable that they should return to their districts immediately."

They were directed to report at their schools tomorrow morning, but it was emphasised that the notification did not mean that "evacuation is to take place."

"If evacuation should become necessary," the broadcast added, "full notice will be given and everyone concerned will be told what to do." 25.8.39

MR. CHAMBERLAIN in Parliament: "Since the House last met the international situation has deteriorated until today we find ourselves confronted with the imminent peril of war. Catastrophe has not yet come upon us. It is, therefore, still hoped that reason and sanity may find a way to reassert themselves. . . . Peace or war does not rest with us. I hope that those on whom the responsibility does rest will think of the millions of human beings whose fate depends upon their action."

PRESIDENT ROOSEVELT in personal peace appeal to King of Italy: "The Governments of Italy and the United States can today advance those ideals of Christianity which of late seem too often to have been obscured. The unheard voices of countless millions of human beings ask that they shall not vainly be sacrificed again."

POPE PIUS XII. (in a world broadcast): "A grave hour is about to sound for the great European family . . . Justice cannot be obtained through violence. Men must try to reason out problems. War is futile. 25.8.39

On that very first day of the war, air-raid sirens wailed in Birmingham as they did in London and other places, but it was a false alarm. The next day, RAF bombers raided the entrance to the Kiel Canal and attacked German warships. The Germans retaliated with a raid on Scotland when a rabbit was reported as the only casualty.

Russian troops complicated matters by crossing the Polish border along its whole length and met up with German troops at Brest Litovst.

Here, in Birmingham and nationwide, cinemas and theatres closed and sporting fixtures were curtailed for fear of bombing, but regulations were soon relaxed. Never mind - we still had Sandy Macpherson at the organ on the wireless. We also had regular doses of 'Band Wagon' with Arthur Askey and 'Hi, Gang!' with Bebe Daniels and Ben Lyon.

The situation became known as 'The Phoney War'; nothing seemed to be happening. Reconnaissance patrols were made by our troops, the French were ensconced behind their Maginot Line and the Germans behind their Siegfried Line. It was all quiet on the Western Front.

At sea, however, we suffered two mighty blows. On 17th September the aircraft carrier 'Courageous' was sunk in the Bristol Channel after a hundred-to-one chance encounter with a U-boat. Out of a crew of 1,260, over 500 were drowned. Then, on 14th October, at 1.30am, a German U-boat braved tides and currents to penetrate our seemingly safe harbour at Scapa Flow in the Orkney Isles and sank our battle-ship 'Royal Oak' whilst she was at anchor. 786 officers and men perished. We were able to redress the situation somewhat on 17th December when, after a running battle with our cruisers 'Exeter', 'Ajax' and 'Achilles', the German pocket-battleship 'Admiral Graf Spee' scuttled herself at the entrance to Montevideo harbour, Uraguay. Her captain, Langsdorff, committed suicide.

In Birmingham, corrugated steel Anderson shelters had been delivered to many households for erection in gardens. Sometimes parts were missing or bolts inferior, but when assembled and ramparted with soil, they were life-savers to many families. An indoor shelter, the Morrison, was sent to houses with no gardens. This shelter was no more than a heavy kitchen table made of steel with strong wire sides, capable of holding up the ruins of a small house. They served their purpose well.

As Christmas approached, the Russo-Finnish war continued unabated, Russia having rejected the League of Nations offer of mediation.

Here, at home, we prepared for the Festive Season. Food rationing

BRITAIN'S FIRST DAY OF WAR: CHURCHILL IS NEW NAVY CHIEF

BRITAIN AND GERMANY HAVE BEEN AT WAR SINCE ELEVEN O'CLOCK YESTERDAY MORNING. FRANCE AND GERMANY HAVE BEEN AT WAR SINCE YESTERDAY AT 5 P.M.

A British War Cabinet of nine members was set up last night. Mr. Winston Churchill, who was First Lord of the Admiralty when Britain last went to war, returns to that post.

Full list of the War Cabinet is:—

PRIME MINISTER: Mr. Neville Chamberlain.
CHANCELLOR OF THE EXCHEQUER: Sir John Simon.
FOREIGN SECRETARY: Viscount Halifax.
DEFENCE MINISTER: Lord Chatfield.
FIRST LORD: Mr. Winston Churchill.
SECRETARY FOR WAR: Mr. Leslie Hore-Belisha.
SECRETARY FOR AIR: Sir Kingsley Wood.
LORD PRIVY SEAL: Sir Samuel Hoare.
MINISTER WITHOUT PORTFOLIO: Lord Hankey.

There are other Ministerial changes. Mr. Eden becomes Dominions Secretary, Sir Thomas Inskip goes to the House of Lords as Lord Chancellor, Lord Stanhope, ex-First Lord, becomes Lord President of the Council, Sir John Anderson is the Home Secretary and Minister of Home Security—a new title.

had not yet begun, but those who could remember the privations of the First World War were insistent its introduction could not be long delayed.

It was a stay-at-home Christmas for petrol rationing had begun on 23rd September. But we still celebrated for, after all, hadn't we been 'Digging for Victory' and growing our own vegetables and fruit?

WANTED!

FOR MURDER . . . FOR KIDNAPPING . . . FOR THEFT AND FOR ARSON

Can be recognised full face by habitual scowl. Rarely smiles. Talks rapidly, and when angered screams like a child.

ADOLF HITLER

ALIAS

Adolf Schicklegruber, Adolf Hittler or Hidler

Last heard of in Berlin, September 3, 1939. Aged fifty, height 5ft. 8½in., dark hair, frequently brushes one lock over left forehead. Blue eyes. Sallow complexion, stout build, weighs about 11st. 3lb. Suffering from acute monomania, with periodic fits of melancholia. Frequently bursts into tears when crossed. Harsh, guttural voice, and has a habit of raising right hand to shoulder level. **DANGEROUS!**

Profile from a recent photograph. Black moustache. Jowl inclines to fatness. Wide nostrils. Deep-set, menacing eyes.

HIS MAJESTY'S BROADCAST

The following message was broadcast by the King from Buckingham Palace throughout the Empire at 6 o'clock last evening:

In this grave hour, perhaps the most fateful in our history, I send to every household of my peoples, both at home and overseas, this message, spoken with the same depth of feeling for each one of you as if I were able to cross your threshold and speak to you myself.

For the second time in the lives of most of us we are at war. Over and over again we have tried to find a peaceful way out of the differences between ourselves and those who are now our enemies. But it has been in vain.

We have been forced into a conflict. For we are called, with our Allies, to meet the challenge of a principle which, if it were to prevail, would be fatal to any civilised order in the world.

It is the principle which permits a State, in the selfish pursuit of power, to disregard its treaties and its solemn pledges; which sanctions the use of force, or threat of force, against the Sovereignty and independence of other States.

Such a principle, stripped of all disguise, is surely the mere primitive doctrine that might is right; and if this principle were established throughout the world, the freedom of our own country and of the whole British Commonwealth of Nations would be in danger.

But far more than this — the peoples of the world would be kept in the bondage of fear, and all hopes of settled peace and of the security of justice and liberty among nations would be ended.

This is the ultimate issue which confronts us. For the sake of all that we ourselves hold dear, and of the world's order and peace, it is unthinkable that we should refuse to meet the challenge.

It is to this high purpose that I now call my people at home and my peoples across the Seas, who will make our cause their own.

I ask them to stand calm, firm and united in this time of trial. The task will be hard. There may be dark days ahead, and war can no longer be confined to the battlefield. But we can only do the right as we see the right, and reverently commit our cause to God.

If one and all we keep resolutely faithful to it, ready for whatever service or sacrifice it may demand, then, with God's help, we shall prevail.

May He bless and keep us all.

"NOW! WHERE'S THAT BLOKE HITLER !!"

Don't Let Your Radio Blare

The B.B.C. appeals to listeners on behalf of night workers.

"Will listeners please remember," they ask, "that, in the house or flat next to them, there may be someone who has been working all night and who has to sleep during the day.

"Will they, therefore, see that the volume of noise from their wireless sets is as little as conveniently possible."

A.R.P. NEEDS MORE MEN

THE need of volunteers for the auxiliary fire service and for stretcher bearer or first-aid parties was emphasised in a statement by the Lord Privy Seal on National Service.

The Lord Privy Seal writes:—

"As already announced, apart from some immediate vacancies for skilled and semi-skilled tradesmen, the Army has practically all the men that it can handle for the present. Men will be called upon when they are needed.

"Those who are engaged in some reserved occupation or in other work obviously of national importance at this time can help the country best by keeping on with their work and keeping the national machine running.

Civil Defence Needs

"There will, however, be many who are not so engaged. For men over twenty there is open the whole field of the Civil Defence services and they can rest assured that, if they enrol now for one or other of these Services, although later the call may come to join the fighting ranks, they will in the meantime, until that call comes be able to render an effective period of service to the country.

"Men are still needed in particular for the auxiliary fire service and for stretcher-bearer or first-aid parties.

"You can enrol for these services through the nearest Employment Exchange or, in the case of fire, at the nearest fire brigade station."

Preparing for the blackout, shades are fitted to red lamps at street islands.

Further blackout preparations, as white squares are painted on kerbstones,
Coventry Road, September.

Local girls evacuated to Pipewood Camp School,
near Rugeley.

No matter how black the outlook there was always a ray of sunshine.

In this case a cinema notice raised a laugh. This picture appeared in the Evening Despatch of September 6 1939.

The caption said: Birmingham's humour, at all times dominant in times of stress, was uppermost in this picture taken outside one of the city's leading cinemas.

Barrage balloons, designed to make flying hazardous
for German planes, leave a hangar, September.

Volunteer messengers ready to work as part of
the Auxiliary Fire Service, 6th September.

10

DON'T . . .

THIS is intended for YOU. Read it, remember it, pass it on to your friends. First, and most important of all things is

Don't Listen
to Rumours

You will get all the news that matters—bad or good—in your newspapers. Disbelieve anything else you hear — particularly alarmist news. Next thing to remember is

Don't Broadcast
Information

You may know that there is an anti-aircraft gun cunningly concealed in the field next to your garden. But that's no reason for passing on the information. It may reach someone who should not know it.

Don't Lose
Your Head

IN OTHER WORDS—KEEP SMILING. THERE'S NOTHING TO BE GAINED BY GOING ABOUT WITH THE CORNERS OF YOUR MOUTH TURNED DOWN, AND IT HAS A BAD EFFECT ON PEOPLE WHOSE NERVES ARE NOT SO GOOD AS YOURS.

SO EVEN IF A BOMB FALLS IN YOUR STREET—WHICH IS UNLIKELY—KEEP SMILING.

Don't Listen
to Scaremongers

You will always find scaremongers about. Just treat them as you would a smallpox case—move on quickly. The enemy loves to spread rumours. Part of his campaign was to panic Britain—and he will still try it, hopeless although it is.

Don't Cause Crowds
to Assemble

THE POLICE HAVE ENOUGH TO DO. IF YOU SEE PEOPLE GATHERING AND THERE IS NO REASON FOR YOU TO JOIN THEM—WALK ON. IN OTHER WORDS—MIND YOUR OWN BUSINESS.

AND ABOVE ALL DON'T FORGET THE OLD ARMY ADAGE.

Be silent, be discreet, enemy ears are listening to you.

NOW GET AHEAD, DO YOUR JOB AND DON'T WORRY.

Filling sandbags, north siding, Bournville, September.

Now where does this piece go? Checking the sections of an Anderson shelter. A typical scene in many a back garden.

As a protection against bombs sandbagging has been placed around the College of Arts and Crafts, Cornwall Street, October.

Air-raid practice, Joseph Lucas Ltd.,
Great King Street, Hockley.

All present and correct. WAAFS (Women's Auxiliary Air Force) at a barrage balloon site.

ARP (Air Raid Precaution) wardens, Yardley.

Women Drivers Free Men for the War

More and more women drivers are coming forward to play their part in the nation's war work. They are releasing men who are called up and men wanted in more vital industries.

Mickey Mouse Masks

Special "Mickey Mouse" gas-masks in various colours and having separate eye-pieces and a little nose are being made for small children who are repelled by the ordinary ones.

Dogs Welcome

British dog-lovers are posting on their gates copies of a notice issued by the National Canine Defence League: "You are not allowed to take your dog into an air-raid shelter, but both you and your canine friend are welcome here when a warning is given."

Ambulance drivers and assistants in their gasproof suits, Birmingham
First Central Reserve Ambulance Depot, Municipal Car Park.

~ MR. CHURCHILL YESTERDAY : ~

I feel, after the ninth week of war, so far as the sea is concerned— and the sea has often proved decisive in the end—we may cherish good hopes that all will be well.

..Shoot straight, Lady

You've got a fighting job on hand, too. These are significant days and anyone — man, woman, or child — who is less than fighting fit is a pull back on the total war effort.

FOOD is your munition of war. The Government sees that you get the right stuff and it's vital that you should know how to use it to full advantage . . .

There's cheese : it makes muscle and bone.

There are potatoes : they give energy and warmth.

Carrots, that give vitality and help you to see in the dark.

Green vegetables, with their valuable salts and vitamins, which are so very important for clear complexions and sound teeth.

Did you know that 5 quarts of summer milk—milk at its richest and when it is most plentiful — go to the making of 1 lb. cheese ?

Or that swedes, the juice of which you used to give to babies because of its valuable Vitamin C, are now to be had at most greengrocers cheap enough and in big enough quantities for you to serve as a second or third vegetable to the entire family ?

All good live stuff. And you need them all : *every day.* Serve everything appetisingly as you so well can do. Then you can be proud of your vital, active part in the drive to Victory.

With their name tags and gas masks the children set off on their evacuation journey.

10 of the best!

K4's

...BETTER-THAN-EVER REAL VIRGINIA CIGARETTES

Kensitas *Cigarettes Sir* REAL VIRGINIA

10 for 7½d

4 & 20—1s 5d

DUTY FREE FOR THE B.E.F.   120 for 3/3 · 240 for 5/9   ASK YOUR RETAILER

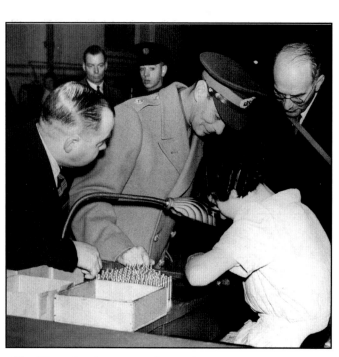

The King checks a cartridge-making operation, Kynoch Ltd., Perry Barr, 27th October.

THE VOLUNTARY white painting of kerbs, lamp-posts, tree trunks and similar obstacles by those who live in suburban roads, is urged by the Chief Constable of Birmingham.

"Birmingham Corporation has painted no less than 350 miles of kerb on main road. The amount of labour and the cost of this work is very considerable and it is impossible to extend this kerb painting to residential thoroughfares," the Chief Constable and City Engineer said in a joint statement.

"The Corporation has welcomed any efforts by residents in these roads who are doing a great service to themselves and their neighbours by undertaking the painting of kerbs outside their own houses.

"This applies also to white bands around lamp-posts, trees or other road obstructions. 2/1/40

Snow, an additional hazard, put pressure on transport and householders on what was becoming known as "The Home Front". We were urged to conserve gas and coal. Rationing of food was introduced on 8th January, beginning with sugar, butter and bacon. Many other items were to follow. The early months of blacked-out windows, street lights and car headlamps made for a gloomy outlook, yet many people said at the outset: "It'll be all over by Christmas". They were saying that in August 1914 too. Little did we know how long and grim the war would be.

The German war machine was driving relentlessly ahead. BLITZKRIEG (literally 'lightning war') was on everyone's lips. Denmark and Norway fell to Hitler's troops. Holland, Belgium and Luxembourg soon suffered a similar fate. France would be Hitler's next conquest. The British Army on the Continent, severely battered, withdrew to the French port of Dunkirk after a brave rearguard action. Over the period 27th May to 4th June, 299 British warships and 420 other vessels, whilst under constant German attacks, evacuated to England 355,490 officers and men, many without their rifles and ammunition. The weather was heaven-sent and granted a relatively smooth crossing of the Dover Straits. A defeat rightly heralded as a victory.

10th June Italy declared war on Britain and, with the final acceptance of Armistice terms by France on 25th June 1940, we were alone against Germany and her axis partner. Meanwhile, Neville Chamberlain had resigned, to be succeeded, momentously, by Winston Churchill. His new War Secretary, Anthony Eden, broadcast an appeal on the radio for men between the ages of 17 and 65 to enlist for the Local Defence Volunteers (LDV). They would eventually receive uniforms and fire-arms but would be unpaid. Their mission, initially, was to protect locally from the menace of enemy paratroops. They registered in their thousands, some still signing up beyond midnight on that first day. Soon Churchill renamed them The Home Guard.

Hitler's planned invasion of Britain did not materialise, mainly due to the Royal Air Force's successful repulsion of the German Luftwaffe during The Battle of Britain.

German bombers, however, continued their attacks unabated. For the rest of 1940, Birmingham was pounded by massive air-raids. London and other cities suffered similarly.

THIS EMPIRE fights on to final victory. We, in this island, working, planning, and fighting as one, can never be defeated. Remember, the strongest armed force that can be brought against us can be outnumbered, outfought and utterly destroyed upon our soil. Meantime, there grows behind us, stronger and stronger with every hour, a mightier armament than the world has ever seen. From our Dominions, from America, no less than from our own factories, will flow —are flowing—tanks, guns, aircraft and equipment for the offensive yet to come. Our food, our trade, our credits, are secure. But upon the enemy who in his turn, must face *our* attack, the strain of war will take increasing toll. Be of good courage.

Work, fight and we shall win.

THANKS to the inspiration and energy of a Kings Norton resident and the organising ability of a Birmingham squadron leader, men in the British Forces, manning our home defences, are likely to find living conditions far more comfortable and homely in the near future.

Not very long after the outbreak of war Mr. Arthur Hackett, of Rednal Road, Kings Norton hit on the idea of inducing residents in his suburb to adopt some of the huts in which men of the local balloon barrage were housed.

It was intended to brighten conditions in which these men were existing.

A reporter described one of the Kings Norton huts . . . a home from home atmosphere pervaded a hut completely fitted out with modern housing amenities.

In one corner stood an old-fashioned but very serviceable sideboard which had been "scrounged" as part of the adoption idea.

There were a brand new card table with packs of cards on hand, any amount of reading materials, periodicals, magazines and books, and tubular steel chairs, which would have been a credit to any hotel lounge.

Birmingham Mail

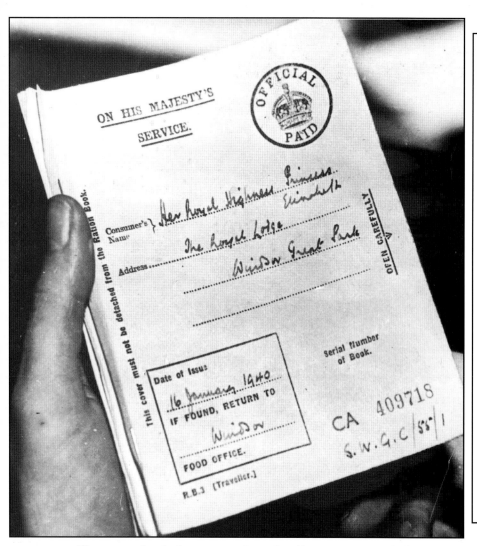

This ration book shows just what a leveller wartime can be!

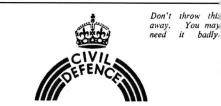

Lord Nuffield oversees work on aeroplane parts,
Castle Bromwich Aeroplane Factory, March.

SPAM — JAM — or SCRAM!!!

HELP YOUR FUEL WATCHER ★

★ That's right — if the job's done TURN OFF THE STEAM

SAVE FUEL AT WORK
ISSUED BY THE MINISTRY OF FUEL & POWER

Auxiliary Fire Service and Police personnel test their agility, Digbeth.

Gas mask drill, Digbeth Police Station.

The King and Queen, on their tour of the city, stop to look at air machine gun parts, BSA (The Birmingham Small Arms Co. Ltd.) Small Heath, 18th April.

A welcome from the employees of the Wolseley works of Morris Motors Ltd., Ward End.

On to Calthorpe Park to see an ARP exercise.

...and then, the next day, to an RAF training centre.

Also finding time for a balloon centre.

Singing star, Jessie Matthews, sings "For the Forces" in the NAAFI show at 6.45pm. After a career consisting of stage, film, radio and recording work, she eventually became Mrs Dale in the long-running radio serial "Mrs Dale's Diary" (1963-1969).

RADIO

HOME SERVICE

767 Kc (391.1 M.) and 868 Kc (449.1 M.)

6.45 A.M.—News in Norwegian. 7—Time, News. 7.15 app.—Violin Solos, played by Nancy Phillips. 7.30—Physical Exercises (younger men). 7.40—Physical Exercises (older women). 7.55—Thought for today. 8—Time, News. 8.15—London Dances to Harry Roy (gramophone). 9—Sunderland Constabulary Band. 9.30—Piano Music, played by Norman Anderson. 10—The Voice of the Nazi—8. Changing the Tune.

10.15—Time, Service. 10.30—H. Robinson Cleaver: Cinema Organ.

11—Schools: Singing together (ages 9-15). 11.25—World History (ages 9-12). 11.45—Senior English (ages 11-15).

12—B.B.C. Northern Orchestra. 12.30—Variety. Half an hour with Trudi Binar, Joan Miller and Evel Burns.

1—Time, News. 1.15—Henry Hall and his Orchestra. 2—Schools: Gardening. 2.20—Preparatory Concert broadcasts (ages 9-15). 2.45—English for under-nines. Action stories and plays.

3—Music for Piano and Strings, played by Norbert Wethmar Piano Quintet. 3.40—Scottish Dance Music: B.B.C. Scottish Orchestra. 4—The North Country Woman—17: Monthly miscellany.

4.25—Tea-time Cabaret, with Frank Titterton, Leslie Weston, Renee Barr, Tiny Powell, Peter Valerio, Thelma Jagger and Leonardi and his Orchestra. 5—News (Welsh). 5.5—The Organ Blower—a story (Welsh). 5.20—Children's Hour. 5.45—The Zoo Man.

6—Time, News. 6.15—Dando at the Organ. 6.30—News in Norwegian.

6.45—White Velvet, by Sax Rohmer: Serial play—Episode 4. 7.5—Reserved for Talks that cannot be announced in advance. 7.15—Announcements. 7.30—Ivor Moreton and Dave Kaye—Tiger Ragamuffins

7.45—The Economic War: What it means to us—10, by Donald Tyerman, dealing with the economic effects of the extension of the war to Holland and Belgium

8—Monday Night at Eight. Inspector Hornleigh, with S. J. Warmington. Anniversary—Memories of famous first nights Puzzle Corner; Elisabeth Welch. Mr. Walker Wants to Know, this week Syd Walker will deal with a poser of John Snagge's. May We Introduce . . .? compered by Davy Burnaby; Singing Commeres the Three Chimes; B.B.C. Variety Orchestra.

9—Time, News. 9.20—Family Allowances: Discussion between Lady Bank and Herbert S. Elvin, a mother of six, and a skilled craftsman. John Hilton in the chair. 9.55—B.B.C. Scottish Orchestra.

10.30—Henry Hall and his Orchestra. 11—The Finest Stories in the World: Esther, produced by Val Gielgud; narrator, Felix Aylmer, with Ronald Simpson, Malcolm Keen, Abraham Sofner, Ann Firth. 11.30—Teddy Wilson—records.

12—Time, News. 12.20 a.m.—News in Norwegian.

FOR THE FORCES

10.58 A.M.—Bow Bells. 11—Time Summary; Organ. 11.30—Casino Trio.

12—Ralph Silvester, with Victor Silvester's Harmony Music (gramophone). 12.30—Home Service.

1—Time: News. 1.15—Home Service.

2—Ransome and Marles Works Band. 2.40—Over to You; Variety, with Jimmy Donovan (saxophone), Barney Johnson (Black-country stories) and Jack Hill (piano).

3—Medvedeff's Balalaika Orchestra. 3.20—Eric Lord at the organ. 3.40—Home Service.

4—Swing It! (gramophone). 4.25—Home Service.

5—Manchester Hippodrome Orchestra. 5.30—Welsh Rarebit: Variety.

6—Foreign Languages Bulletin. 6.30—Close-Up, Leslie Mitchell interviews Jean Gillie and Hartley Power.

6.45—Drury Lane Calling: NAAFI presents ENSA half-hour, with Jessie Matthews, Sonnie Hale, Stanley Holloway and Geraldo and his Orchestra: ENSA discovery from the Forces—Naomi Jacob in the Voice of B.E.F.; Community singing recorded by troops somewhere in England; Robert Montgomery (guest compere), from stage of Theatre Royal, Drury Lane.

7.15—Dear Old Southland: Programme of dance music styled the ultra-modern way, featuring Ken Johnson and his West Indian Dance Orchestra, with Betty Kent, Al Bowlly, Don Johnson and the Johnsonairs.

8—Home Service. 9—Foreign Languages. 9.15—What's on Tomorrow?

9.20—Sim Grossman and his Dance Band. 9.45—Canadian News-Letter.

10—Featherweight Boxing: Southern Area Championship—Jackie Rankin (Southall) v. Billie Walker (Stratford); commentary. 10.50—A Night with Paul Whiteman at the Biltmore (records).

11 P.M.—Home Service.

Winston Churchill takes over, as Prime Minister, from the ailing Neville Chamberlain, 10th May.

An ARP despatch rider about to set off.

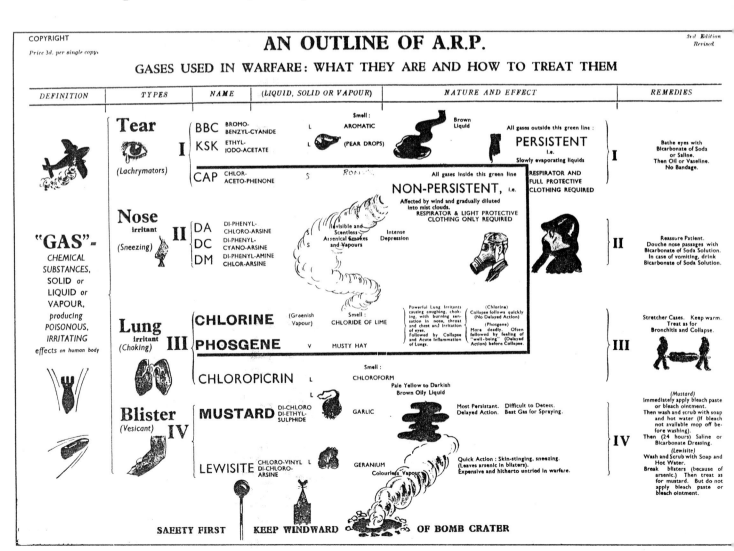

3rd Edition
Revised

AN OUTLINE OF A.R.P.

GASES USED IN WARFARE: WHAT THEY ARE AND HOW TO TREAT THEM

DEFINITION	TYPES	NAME	(LIQUID, SOLID OR VAPOUR)	NATURE AND EFFECT	REMEDIES
"GAS" = CHEMICAL SUBSTANCES, SOLID or LIQUID or VAPOUR, producing POISONOUS, IRRITATING effects on human body	**Tear** (Lachrymators) I	BBC BROMO-BENZYL-CYANIDE	L — Smell: AROMATIC	Brown Liquid. All gases outside this green line: **PERSISTENT** i.e. Slowly evaporating liquids	I — Bathe eyes with Bicarbonate of Soda or Saline. Then Oil or Vaseline. No Bandage.
		KSK ETHYL-IODO-ACETATE	L (PEAR DROPS)		
		CAP CHLOR-ACETO-PHENONE	S	All gases inside this green line **NON-PERSISTENT**, i.e. Affected by wind and gradually diluted into mist clouds. RESPIRATOR & LIGHT PROTECTIVE CLOTHING ONLY REQUIRED	RESPIRATOR AND FULL PROTECTIVE CLOTHING REQUIRED
	Nose irritant (Sneezing) II	DA DI-PHENYL-CHLORO-ARSINE; DC DI-PHENYL-CYANO-ARSINE; DM DI-PHENYL-AMINE CHLOR-ARSINE	S Invisible and Scentless Arsenical Smokes and Vapours. Intense Depression		II — Reassure Patient. Douche nose passages with Bicarbonate of Soda Solution. In case of vomiting, drink Bicarbonate of Soda Solution.
	Lung irritant (Choking) III	**CHLORINE**	(Greenish Vapour) Smell: CHLORIDE OF LIME	Powerful Lung Irritants causing coughing, choking, with burning sensation in nose, throat and chest and Irritation of eyes. Followed by Collapse and Acute Inflammation of Lungs. (Chlorine) Collapse follows quickly (No Delayed Action)	III — Stretcher Cases. Keep warm. Treat as for Bronchitis and Collapse.
		PHOSGENE	V MUSTY HAY	(Phosgene) More deadly. Often followed by feeling of "well-being" (Delayed Action) before Collapse.	
		CHLOROPICRIN	L Smell: CHLOROFORM	Pale Yellow to Darkish Brown Oily Liquid	
	Blister (Vesicant) IV	**MUSTARD** DI-CHLORO DI-ETHYL-SULPHIDE	Smell: GARLIC	Most Persistant. Difficult to Detect. Delayed Action. Best Gas for Spraying.	IV — (Mustard) Immediately apply bleach paste or bleach ointment. Then wash and scrub with soap and hot water (If bleach not available mop off before washing). Then (24 hours) Saline or Bicarbonate Dressing. (Lewisite) Wash and Scrub with Soap and Hot Water. Break blisters (because of arsenic) Then treat as for mustard. But do not apply bleach paste or bleach ointment.
		LEWISITE CHLORO-VINYL DI-CHLORO-ARSINE	L Smell: GERANIUM Colourless Vapour	Quick Action: Skin-stinging, sneezing. (Leaves arsenic in blisters). Expensive and hitherto untried in warfare.	

SAFETY FIRST | KEEP WINDWARD OF BOMB CRATER

You Must Carry Your Gas Mask

A.R.P. Should Be On Alert

—Says Ministry

The Minister of Home Security states that in the light of to-day's events in Holland and Belgium, it is very necessary that all civil defence and A.R.P. services should be on the alert.

The carrying of gas masks by the public is once more necessary. They should acquaint themselves with the position of shelters and first aid post in their neighbourhoods.

Householders are recommended to overhaul their domestic preparations against air attack.

10.5.40

LEN HARVEY the holder of the British and Empire Heavyweight championship will give three exhibition bouts at the Tower Ballroom, Birmingham on May 20 in aid of the Lord Mayor's War Relief Fund.

This will be Harvey's first appearance in the boxing ring in Birmingham and as he is serving in the RAF he has had to be specially released for the occasion.

A warden fits a contex to a civilian respirator, 22nd May. This was an additional filter to give protection against arsenical smokes.

ITALY IS TO-DAY AT WAR WITH FRANCE AND BRITAIN, AFTER EIGHT HOURS' NOTICE OF HER DECISION.

At 4 p.m. yesterday Count Ciano informed the Allied Ambassadors in Rome that Italy would enter the war on the side of Germany at midnight.

At 6 o'clock Mussolini proclaimed to a war-fevered crowd that Italy had made her "irrevocable" decision.

IT WAS MET BY THE FIRMEST REPLIES BOTH FROM LONDON AND PARIS. IN LONDON IT WAS OFFICIALLY STATED THAT THE ALLIES KNEW HOW TO MEET SWORD WITH SWORD.

PRESIDENT ROOSEVELT, BROADCASTING EARLY TO-DAY, REVEALED THAT MUSSOLINI HAD TURNED DOWN HIS OFFER TO MEDIATE ON ITALY'S CLAIMS, AND SAID THAT HE HAD GIVEN THE ORDER "FULL SPEED AHEAD" FOR ARMAMENTS FOR THE ALLIES.

Violent fighting was continuing last night along the whole Weygand Line, and Paris was placed in a state of defence as the Germans were reported across the Lower Seine at certain points.

11.6.40

New Low Record For Conchies

The 1910 class, who registered yesterday, provided a new low record for conscientious objectors. Out of a provisional total of 332,995, objectors numbered only 2,291—.69 per cent.

In England 283,268 men registered, in Scotland 32,692, and in Wales 17,035. The registrations bring the total to more than 2,800,000. The four additional group registrations to be effected next month will raise that figure to about 4,000,000.

Many men who will fill specialised jobs in the Services were among those who registered at Labour Exchanges throughout the country yesterday.

Garage Workers Are Wanted For Plane Factories

Lord Beaverbrook, Minister of Aircraft Production, has appealed to garage workers to volunteer as fitters in aircraft factories.

"The most urgent need of this hour," it was officially stated, "is a great increase in the output of aeroplanes."

Volunteers for this work of highest national importance are asked to go to the nearest aircraft factory or Employment Exchange.

21

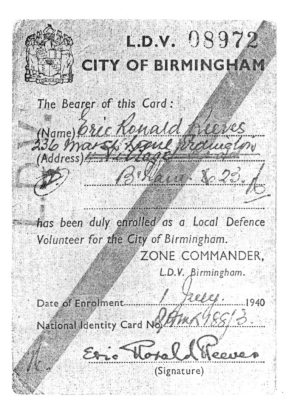

Local Defence Volunteers (known afterwards as The Home Guard)
drill with wooden rifles.

Officers of B Co., 27th Warks. (Birmingham) Bn., Home Guard, on manoeuvres.

Cadbury's works' fire brigade tackling an incendiary device.

Pots, pans, kettles and everything suitable is collected, in the drive to re-cycle aluminium to help the war effort. Sadly, some of the sacrificed objects turned out to be totally unsuitable!

A bigger ARMY NEEDS A bigger Y.M.C.A

DON'T LET OUR LOSSES IN FRANCE HANDICAP US TODAY

More huts, centres and mobile canteens are urgently required on the NEW HOME FRONT. The 550 centres now operating in Britain are not enough.

The need of the fighting forces for the Y.M.C.A. has never been greater than NOW.

BUT—in standing by the B.E.F., the Y.M.C.A. has lost heavily. To meet the needs of the Navy, Army and Air Force TODAY these losses have to be made good.

The Y.M.C.A. has served the troops in Flanders, on the quay at Boulogne, on the beaches at Dunkirk—through Normandy to Brittany it has been with the B.E.F. during these last weeks. Y.M.C.A. workers have met the returning B.E.F., dispensing *free* hundreds of thousands of cigarettes, thousands of gallons of tea, tons of food. Help us to help the men who defend our shores. £200,000 urgently needed to complete the first £500,000. Even if you can only send a few shillings or coppers, you will be helping more than you realise.

This is the estimate at present available of our losses in France:

The Equipment and Stores of 37 Centres

The Contents of Four Stores Depots and Four Railway Truck Loads of Stores

A Group of Permanent Buildings

15 Huts · 24 Mobile Canteens

5 Lorries and 12 Cars

20 Marquees and 30 Smaller Tents

DEFENCE REGULATIONS

To _Mr E. J. Howd_
(Name)

Occupier of _26 Almyock Road._
(Address)

THIS NOTICE IS TO GIVE YOU PRELIMINARY WARNING that in certain circumstances it may become necessary to require you to provide, in the premises above-mentioned, accommodation for _2_ persons (in general Civil Servants). Should it be decided to require this accommodation, a Billeting Notice will be served upon you under Regulation 22 of the Defence Regulations, 1939, and every endeavour will be made to give you as long notice as possible. Circumstances, however, may arise under which it will not be practicable to give you more than twenty-four hours' notice, and it has therefore been thought desirable to notify you of this possibility in advance.

Signed _H. K. Collyer_
Billeting Officer authorised by the Minister of Health

Date___17 / 7___1940.

80m 10/39—[6159] G663 10m 5/40 15403 G & S 704

Plane Trap Is Secret

A PLANE trap erected by the Ministry of Transport caught a German bomber yesterday and wrecked it.

All the crew were killed.

British military authorities have no intention of giving away to the enemy details of the plane trap.

The trap is the latest British "hush-hush" defence weapon, as the Nazis have already learned to their cost.

More news of its formidable and effective nature can be expected soon.

16.8.40

Birmingham children being medically examined, prior to overseas evacuation, 2nd July.

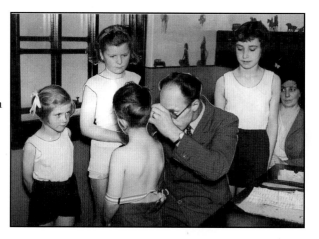

One of the city's most famous sights, the Market Hall Clock. The Market Hall, itself, was gutted in the raids of 25th/26th August.

Certificate of Official Recognition
granted by the Admiralty, War Office, and Air Ministry to affiliated Voluntary Organizations.

This is to Certify that

MRS. SPENCER'S GROUP OF WORKERS
REGISTERED NO. WARWICK/W/258
ATTACHED TO
THE LORD MAYOR OF BIRMINGHAM'S WAR RELIEF FUND

is officially recognised under the Scheme for co-ordinating the national voluntary effort in providing comforts for His Majesty's Combatant Forces and may use with its title the words " Approved by the Admiralty, War Office and Air Ministry."

Dated this 23rd August, 1940.

Roof spotters out looking for enemy planes, 11th September.

WHATEVER'S IN HIS POCKETS, YOU MAY WANT IT, INTELLIGENCE NEED IT ! HAND IT OVER

IN BIRMINGHAM, as in other parts of the country, a new form of patriotic activity is being organised by the Women's Voluntary Services for Civil Defence.

The object is to satisfy the desire of many housewives to play their part in national service outside the existing organisations, which their home duties do not permit them to join.

This "Housewives Service" aims to assist the air raid wardens from inside the home but without interfering with their work.

FIRE WATCHERS will begin training in Birmingham next week.

It is now compulsory for all factories and works to employ a trained watchman who will be on duty at night to guard against fire.

This step was taken by the Home Office because it was appreciated that neglect in dealing with an incendiary bomb may lead to a serious fire.

Staff at the First Aid Post, Kent Street Baths, September.

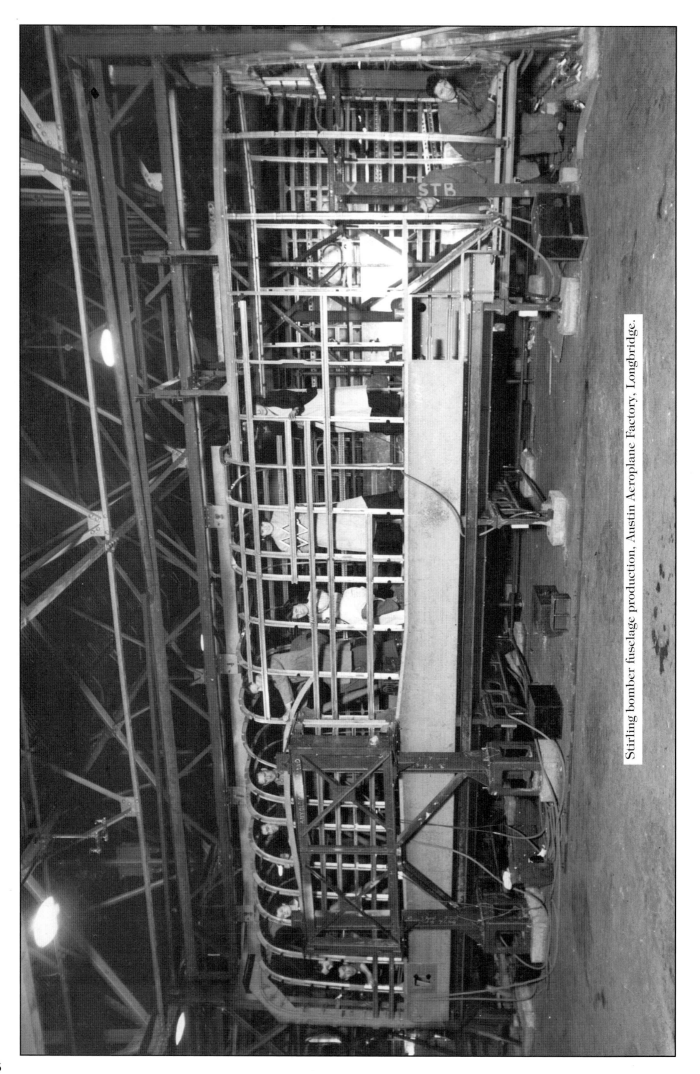

Stirling bomber fuselage production, Austin Aeroplane Factory, Longbridge.

Food Hints Shop, 125/6 New Street, October.

HOME GUARDS—

Beware of Hitler's unseen ally!—rheumatism

LAST winter you spent your nights in your own warm bed. Now you spend your nights in coldness, wind and rain. Watch out for rheumatism!

It is easy to make light of the first assaults of this old foe of the human race. What are a few aches and twinges to a man who is serving his country? But once rheumatism gets a grip on you, it will take months, or even years, to drive it out.

Rheumatism is one of those illnesses which should be nipped in the bud. Drive it out before it can secure a hold. Clear the poisons out of your system with the help of Kruschen, with its special Double Action, diuretic as well as aperient. In this way you will save yourself years

of suffering and incapacity. If you have already allowed rheumatism to get a strong grip on your system, then go to your doctor at once. Almost certainly you will find that he will prescribe Kruschen as part of your treatment.

But if rheumatism is just making its first attacks on you—take Double Action Kruschen. Take a teaspoonful in hot water, first thing every morning. It's a stitch in time which will save you much misery and expense in the years to come.

Kruschen costs you only 1/9, 1/- and 6d. (subject to Purchase Tax) from any chemist.

IF you drink four cups of tea a day, do you think you could get along with three? . . . or, on a more proportionate basis, do you think you could reduce your tea-drinking by one-fourth?

The Ministry of Food points out that every possible ton of shipping is needed for commodities vital to the winning of the war, and that a further 50,000 tons a year would be released if everyone reduced his or her tea-drinking by one cup in four.

"Statistics show that, since the start of the war, the consumption of tea has risen," the DAILY SKETCH was told yesterday. "There is no shortage, but as consumption rises, more supplies will have to be imported."

"Every possible economy should be exercised in order to release the maximum of shipping for other purposes connected with the country's war effort."

A break from fire fighting, L.C. Smith and Corona Typewriters Ltd., Broad Street.

Smallbrook Street and on the left we are urged to buy at pre-war prices, 26th October.
The night before the Empire Theatre, on the corner of Hurst Street, had been badly damaged.

Pupils tidy up at their school.

The Fire Service swings into action, Moseley Street, the morning of 26th October.

Walter Higgs, M.P. for West Birmingham, watches a rescue team at work.

Morrison's praise for Lord Dudley

Mr. Morrison, after his tour, told an *Evening Despatch* reporter:—

"I am impressed with the fact that although Birmingham has had a pretty rough time, nevertheless, the cheerful and heartening thing is that the city still stands and goes on with its production and its daily business."

In heavily-bombed areas, he said, came the test of standing up to the shock of big scale attack. The encouraging thing is that the areas that have had a heavy time have kept their heads.

"If they didn't, if they were shocked off the job, it would be a major disaster. That must not happen; it has not happened, and it will not happen."

Mr. Morrison added that experience had shown that the system of building up A.R.P. organisations from local government had completely vindicated itself.

"What is new is the regional organisation, and in the Midlands area it has done a good job, and I am indebted to Lord Dudley, the Regional Commissioner, and his staff, for the way they have stood up to it.

"They have not had a cake-walk, and they will not have a cake-walk, but they have done and are doing their job well."

Temporary repairs to bomb-damaged windows, Birmingham Co-operative Society Ltd., Marsh Lane, Erdington.

An LMS railway roof spotter keeps watch.

A Heinkel bomber, on show at the Colonnade, fails to divert the children's attention from a crater caused by a bomb, Broad Street.

Hill Street, with the rear of the Futurist Cinema, left of centre, 20th November. The night before had seen a massive raid by 350 bombers.

SUNDAY entertainment at Birmingham cinemas, theatres and music halls will begin at 2.30 p.m. from Sunday next.

A month after fixing 4—9 p.m. permitted hours, the Public Entertainment Committee yesterday amended them to 2.30—8 by a majority decision.

Mr. Arthur Ward, who made the application, said that the cinemas were, in effect, only having one house instead of the two possible because people would not attend for the later house. The first Sunday after the 4 p.m. to 9 p.m. hours were granted, one cinema's takings fell by £100 and another by £200.

The applicants were willing to give an undertaking not to allow children to attend unless accompanied by parent or guardian.

Mr. Charles Henry Russ, vice-chairman of the Birmingham and Midland branch of the C.E.A.; Mr. Leslie Holderness, general manager of the Paramount Theatre; and Mr. Dennis Salberg, of the Alexandra Theatre, gave evidence in support of the application.

19.11.40

Gathering together belongings from wrecked homes, 22nd December.

Little Green Lane,
Small Heath, 28th November.

500,000 *women by next August for the new 'army'.*

By Our Industrial Correspondent

MORE THAN A MILLION NEW WORKERS ARE EXPECTED TO BE ABSORBED INTO MUNITIONS PRODUCTION BEFORE NEXT AUGUST. HALF OF THESE ARE LIKELY TO BE WOMEN.

Restore Signposts

SIR,—Is it not time now to restore at least some of the road signposts? Lorry-drivers and private motorists on urgent business find their work needlessly hampered, and waste much petrol through losing their way, often with the "aid" of intentionally misleading directions.—**L. M. Heler, Henley-in-Arden, near Birmingham.**

Night and day men of the Royal Navy cheerfully risk their lives to guard your food. They don't mind danger but waste gives them the creeps!

"Of course I've saved them—they're bound by law to give me my job back after the war."

No Christmas Bombs?

MAY I, as a mother of three young children, suggest an air-raid truce of three days and nights at Christmas—the Tuesday, Wednesday, and Thursday of Christmas week?

In normal times the Germans make as much of this festival as we do, and I cannot but feel that German mothers must be as anxious as we are in Britain to keep our children out of the shelters and have them safe in the family circle for this brief time.

A three-days bombing truce, then—just for the sake of the children. A MOTHER.

Birmingham soldiers of the Warks. Yeomanry enjoy a short leave, Palestine.

Wives of Cadbury's employees parcelling and despatching goods to the Forces for Christmas.

Britain's war commitments in the Mediterranean and North Africa caught many of the newspaper headlines and reports in 1941. Things started well. In January, Bardia, Tobruk and, in early February, Benghasi, were taken by our troops. The Royal Navy routed the Italian fleet at Cape Matapan. But, by April, Greece had surrendered to the Germans.

At home, heavy air-raids continued to inflict casualties and widespread damage on cities, including Birmingham. National Days of Prayer were held to help stiffen the morale of the civilian population. Rationing became even more stringent. Clothes went on ration in June.

The intriguing arrival of Rudolph Hess, Hitler's deputy, by parachute after piloting an ME110 fighter from Augsburg to Scotland on 10th May, grabbed just about all the headlines. Hess, who idolised Hitler, hoped to negotiate peace terms as a special gift for his beloved Führer. Imprisonment for life was all that Hess got for his pains.

22nd June was a significant day, for then Germany invaded Russia. Suddenly, Russia was our ally. Things did not go well for the Red Army, but gradually the unrelenting Russian winter played its part and the Germans were halted on 4th December before the very gates of Moscow. The ogre, Joseph Stalin, became "Uncle Joe". Tanks and armaments, some made in Birmingham, became "Tanks for Russia". Chalked on their sides were messages from the workers who had made them: "Have a go, Joe!" - "To hell with Hitler!". British families, deprived though they were, made up parcels of goods for the suffering people in the Soviet Union. "Bundles for Russia" caught on quickly.

Meanwhile, the Home Guard had progressed from being armed with broomsticks and golf-clubs to being equipped with one rifle and two rounds of ammunition between two men. The rumour that they had been issued with pikes in 1940 was false, but pikes were issued in 1941, under Churchill's express orders when he heard that there were some of these ancient arms lying unused in the Tower of London.

A World War became a reality in December when the Japanese attacked the US base at Pearl Harbour. Britain and America declared war on Japan; America declared war on Germany.

The year ended on a dismal note. Two of our capital ships, HMS 'Repulse' and 'Prince of Wales', were sunk off Malaya by the Japanese who proceeded to invade the Philippines. On Christmas Day Hong Kong fell to the Japanese.

Fire watching in the city centre on New Year's Day.

Railway employees form a fire fighting unit.

ARP Consol portable shelters, designed to hold four people, are tested with falling masonry.

An asbestos-clad fire fighter uses a snuffer to put out an incendiary bomb, 25th January.

I saw three ships a-sailing
But not with food for me
For I am eating home-grown foods
To beat the enemy
And ships are filled with guns instead
To bring us Victory

The Birmingham City Corporation saves as much as £30,000 a year in respect of material which would otherwise be wasted on the rubbish-dumps. Particularly welcome during wartime is " any old iron "

MINISTRY OF FOOD
LONDON S.W.1

This is the emblem of the Ministry of Food. It is the banner under which you, too, are fighting ; helping to defeat the enemy's attempt to starve us out.

Through rationing, price control and other measures, the Ministry of Food sees that all get a fair share of essential foods at fair prices.

But nearly half of our food comes across the sea. The U-boats attack our food ships, and although most arrive safely, some are lost.

Now, here is *your* part in the fight for Victory. When a particular food is not available, cheerfully accept something else — home produced if possible. Keep loyally to the rationing regulations.

Above all — whether you are shopping, cooking or eating — remember "FOOD IS A MUNITION OF WAR. DON'T WASTE IT."

Woolton.

MINISTER OF FOOD

WOMEN OF 22 TO REGISTER

300,000 of 21 Clas
Signed On

The second registration c women under the Employmen Order, 1941, was officially ar nounced yesterday. Women bor in the year 1919 will be require to register at a local office of th Ministry of Labour on Satu day week.

Women who were born in 192 to the number of approximatel 300,000, registered yesterday Many of them were already doin essential work, but unless the were in one of the services open t women, they were required to sig on. They were instructed to pr duce their national identity cards.

The Ministry of Labour do n propose to call away from thei employment those at present en gaged in useful work. The regis tration cards of all those who sig will be examined, and in two o three weeks' time those who th Ministry believe may be mor suitably employed will be inter viewed. Experienced wome officers will undertake this task.

SANG FROID

MY mother, brothers and sister were all down the Anderson at the bottom of our garden. It was a very bad night and we had listened to the roars and thuds for some time. Suddenly we heard a long whine, then a terrific thud and our shelter heeled over like a ship. Earth and glass came tumbling over the shelter from the damaged houses, when my brother piped up, "Mum, that's the Howard's greenhouse gone. Won't they be annoyed when they see it in the morning."

Counter-Measures

EVERY recruit to Communism or to the P.P.U. is a potential menace to the security of the country. Why should it be left to the opposition to band themselves into societies for the furtherance of their evil objects? Let us form a "National" or "Patriotic" Society, one of whose objects will be to counteract systematically the underground workings of these wicked forces.—*V. M. V., Birmingham.*

One of the trams destroyed in the raid on Miller Street Depot on the 9th April. It is seen, in happier days, in Dale End.

A Stirling bomber, built at Longbridge, about to leave a runway which is now part of West Works.

Signal Troop, HQ Squadron, Warks. Yeomanry, Palestine. The regiment raised its HQ wing and two sabre troops of B Squadron at Taunton Road Barracks, Sparkbrook. Many of the men joined in groups from such firms as The Britannic Assurance Co.

Jobs a-plenty for the girls.

Pressing jerry can handles, Austin Motor Co.

Worcester Street.

An ambulance train and its team wait to take elderly people out of Birmingham to escape the bombing.

Edgbaston Street, 10th April.

Decontamination and rescue squads at work.

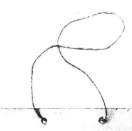

NOTICE

If you wish to be called during an Air Raid kindly hang this card on the handle outside your bedroom door.

JOHN BULL

FREE
AIR RAID
INSURANCE

Underwritten at
LLOYD'S

AND

COMPREHENSIVE
HOUSEHOLD
SECURITY
GIFT

Certificate
of
Registration

FAMOUS LAST WORDS

IT'S ALL RIGHT, LADS—IT'S A BLENHEIM!

From High Street, looking towards Corporation Street.

Thirsty work as the Army clear up after a direct hit on a public house.

The Prime Minister tours bombed areas, giving encouragement to Civil Defence workers and the population in general.

Postal Delays in Wartime

CONSIDERING the difficulties with which the Postmaster-General and his staff have to contend, our letters generally reach us with exemplary promptitude. Mails may, however, be considerably delayed by air raids and other wartime activities, and the Post Office has prepared a stamp of special design which will be impressed on inland correspondence that has been seriously delayed by enemy action. If the delay is slight the stamp will not be used, as this would only cause further delay, perhaps by missing connexion with a delivery. It is about the size of a halfpenny, and shows a bomb enclosed by the words " Delayed by enemy action."

Rescue Squad, made up of employees from W.J. Whittall & Son Ltd. (Builders), Lancaster Street, Aston.

D Co., 27th Warks. Bn., Home Guard, 15th June.

Repairs go on in Steelhouse Lane, after the Chief Constable's office in Newton Street, had been hit, April.

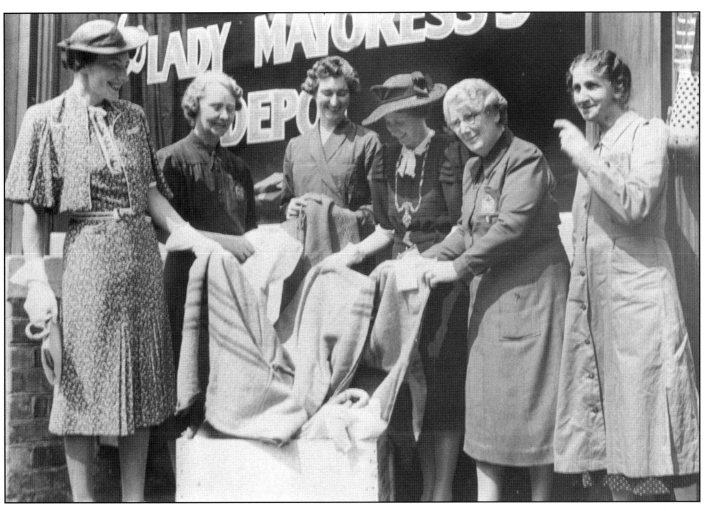

Mrs L.J. Cadbury (left) hands over a consignment of blankets, from her firm's Montreal factory,
to the Lady Mayoress, Mrs Elvira Martineau, July.

The Lord Mayor, Wilfrid Martineau and Regional Commissioner, Lord Dudley, check
an RAF exhibition of photographs, 3rd May.

Yesterday, exactly three weeks after the Prime Minister in one of his most notable broadcasts had assured the nation that the British Government would do everything it could to further practical collaboration with the Government of the Soviet Union bringing about the defeat of Germany, a very important joint declaration was announced simultaneously in London and Moscow.

Its text is terse and emphatic. Each Government will render to the other all the help possible to hasten victory.

14.7.41

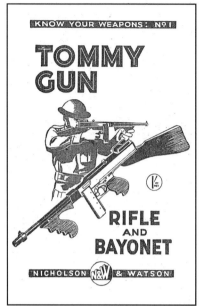

The world's fastest tank, the Crusader, in production, 4th August.

Birmingham Co-operative Society Ltd., High Street, 22nd September.

THERE are many encouraging features in the food production campaign for 1941 supplies.

Owing to the favourable autumn it has been possible to sow a considerably increased acreage of winter wheat, and the young corn is looking strong and healthy. There should be much more wheat to harvest next year.

The beet sugar factories are intensely busy turning out our sugar ration, and the beets now being harvested are proving very rich in sugar.

Also beet contracts for 1941 are being taken up so freely that one or two factories already have been offered more beets than they will be able to handle.

There is every probability that for the second year in succession 1941 will see the whole of the domestic sugar ration (as it now stands) manufactured in our own country.

FIRST details of American losses in the Japanese attack on Pearl Harbour, Hawaii, on Dec. 7, were given by Col. Knox, U.S. Navy Secretary, on his return on Dec. 15 from a visit of investigation. The battleship Arizona was sunk through "a lucky hit"; three destroyers, the Cassin, Downes and Shaw, each of 1,500 tons, were also sunk, together with a minelayer, the Oglala, and an old wireless-controlled target ship, Utah. The battleship Oklahoma capsized, but Col. Knox stated she could be righted and repaired. Casualties among personnel amounted to 2,729 naval officers and men killed and 656 wounded, while Army casualties totalled 168 killed, 223 wounded and 26 missing. Losses in aircraft were severe.

The 39th WARWICKSHIRE BATT. HOME GUARD

present

"OFF PARADE"

A GRAND CONCERT
IN AID OF
BATTALION WELFARE FUND

By kind permission of
Lt.-Col. A. G. COLLEY
Commanding Officer

SUNDAY, DEC. 7, 1941, 3 p.m.
ALEXANDRA THEATRE
JOHN BRIGHT STREET
BIRMINGHAM

On 26th January the first American troops arrived in Britain and at Birmingham's New Street Station their well-tailored uniforms were much in evidence.

Early in this new year the Japanese continued to dominate in south-east Asia. Singapore fell on 15th February. Victory for the Allies seemed a long, long way off. To add to the gloom this month, soap was rationed in Britain.

Admiration for the citizens of Malta culminated in the award of the George Cross to mark the heroic withstanding of the siege. On a lighter note, on 10th February, Glenn Miller, the American band leader, was presented with the world's first golden disc for selling a million copies of "Chattanooga Choo Choo".

A lift for the workers of Birmingham came on 30th May when over 1,000 RAF bombers raided Cologne. This was the first operation of this magnitude in the war so far. Stirling bombers, some made at the Austin Works, took part. Our aircraft followed this by making their first daylight raid on the Ruhr, Germany's heavily defended industrial area.

In June, a morale-boosting visit was made by Mrs Churchill, the Prime Minister's wife, to the YMCA at Handsworth. She always gave her husband tremendous support, ably shown by her appearances at his side on so many of his visits around the country.

Birmingham folk continued to have their sleep disturbed by night-time or early morning air-raid alerts. Many people had become dismissive of these warnings and did not resort to their shelters. The end of July saw the city's final air-raid, as such, although a few stray bombs fell on Bordesley Green during the following April.

Better news was received in August as American forces fought back in the Pacific Ocean theatre of war. As autumn came, the Germans were halted at Stalingrad and British forces began the final push for victory in North Africa. After the Battle of El Alamein, Rommel's troops were in full retreat. Those victory parades and street parties suddenly seemed so much nearer a reality. But there was still a long way to go.

National Savings campaigns were always well supported by the people of Birmingham. Various themes were adopted: "Warship Week", "Salute The Soldier Week", "Wings For Victory Week" and many more. And how the money flowed in!

It was too early yet to countenance the opening of the Second Front (much requested by Stalin) as demonstrated by the ill-fated raid on Dieppe by commando troops. Our Canadian allies suffered heavily.

This year the people of Birmingham would hear for the first time the hit song "White Christmas" and would be enjoying newly-released films such as "Casablanca", "Mrs Miniver" and "In Which We Serve".

Glenn Miller

Home Guard bayonet practice.

Women wardens report for duty. Incidentally, although everyone says there was an acute shortage of film, in wartime, there were literally millions of photographs taken!

Zone Headquarters, Warks. (Birmingham) Home Guard.

In order to protect commercial vehicle petrol from being sold on the black market, or pilfered, a special dye was added. Here, a policemen carries out a test for any such illegal duty-free fuel.

Head and Deputy Head ARP wardens, Duke Street Sub-Division, Aston.

The fall of Singapore was announced by Mr. Churchill in a broadcast last night.

He described the loss of the great naval base and fortress, which cost £30,000,000 to construct, as a "heavy and far-reaching military defeat."

Up to a late hour no details of the capitulation were issued in London. A Tokyo communiqué declared that the Imperial Forces surrendered unconditionally at 7 p.m. Singapore time (12.30 p.m. B.S.T.) yesterday.

The Japanese claim that the surrender was negotiated by the British G.O.C., Lt.-Gen. Percival, and the Japanese commander-in-chief in the Ford works at the foot of Bukit Timah Hill. Preliminary discussions were entered into under a flag of truce.

Berlin radio, quoting a Japanese newspaper, stated that the greater part of the British and Australian forces in Singapore left on Friday for Java in about 30 ships.   16.2.42

The Equator

Behold Ye, *To whom it may concern, particularly the King's enemies, that*

........1221871........ E R REEVES

of the ROYAL AIR FORCE

HAS crossed the Line from the North to the South in the absence of His Majesty Neptunus and His Court.

Therefore I *Adjure all men and women of good will to render unto him or her every assistance in confounding His Majesty's enemies in both Hemispheres.*

Given *Under my hand this ninth day of March in the year Nineteen hundred and forty two, the day of crossing from North to South.*

MASTER.

FIRE WATCHING ROTA FOR HEMYOCK ROAD

April, 1942

		Dusk to 2 a.m.	2 a.m. to Dawn
	1	Dr. and Mrs. Bishop	Mr. and Mrs. Templeman
	2	Mr. and Mrs. Freen	Mr. and Mrs. Best
	3	Mr. and Mrs. Priestnall	Mr. and Mrs. Worth
	4	Mr. and Mrs. Winterton	Mr. and Mrs. Timmins
Sun.	5	Mr. and Mrs. Chinn	Mrs. Painter + Mrs. Smith
	6	Mr. and Mrs. Barker	Mr. and Mrs. Gumbley
	7	Misses Preen	Miss Waterfield + Mrs. Goldby
	8	Mr. and Mrs. Hand	Mr. and Mrs. Templeman
	9	Dr. and Mrs. Bishop	Mr. and Mrs. Best
	10	Mr. and Mrs. Freen	Mr. and Mrs. Worth
	11	Mr. and Mrs. Pohl	Dr. Frankel + Miss Wilkinson
Sun.	12	Mr. and Mrs. Priestnall	Mr. and Mrs. Timmins
	13	Mrs. Painter and Mrs. Smith	Mr. and Mrs. Chinn
	14	Mr. and Mrs. Gumbley	Mr. and Mrs. Barker
	15	Miss Waterfield + Mrs. Goldby	Misses Preen
	16	Mr. and Mrs. Templeman	Mr. and Mrs. Hand
	17	Mr. and Mrs. Best	Dr. and Mrs. Bishop
	18	Mr. and Mrs. Winterton	Dr. Frankel + Miss Wilkinson
Sun.	19	Mr. and Mrs. Pohl	Mr. and Mrs. Timmins
	20	Mr. and Mrs. Worth	Mr. and Mrs. Freen
	21	Mr. and Mrs. Chinn	Mrs. Painter + Mrs. Smith
	22	Mr. and Mrs. Barker	Mr. and Mrs. Gumbley
	23	Misses Preen	Miss Waterfield + Mrs. Goldby
	24	Mr. and Mrs. Hand	Mr. and Mrs. Templeman
	25	Dr. Frankel and Miss Wilkinson	Mr. and Mrs. Winterton
Sun.	26	Dr. and Mrs. Bishop	Mr. and Mrs. Best
	27	Mr. and Mrs. Preen	Mr. and Mrs. Worth
	28	Mr. and Mrs. Priestnall	Mr. and Mrs. Timmins
	29	Mrs. Painter and Mrs. Smith	Mr. and Mrs. Chinn
	30	Mr. and Mrs. Gumbley	Mr. and Mrs. Barker

Please note that the arrangement for the wardens to call the Fire Parties on the alert is no longer in operation and full responsibility for hearing the warning rests with the party on duty.

If you are unable to take part at the time arranged, please arrange for a substitute if possible, or inform Mr. Chinn.

Please let Mr. Chinn know before 26th April which nights in May you will be unable to take part.

The Prime Minister does his "twirling-the-hat-on-a-cane" routine, Civic House, Great Charles Street/Summer Row. The premises housed the offices of the Ministry of Home Security, the ARP Dept. and Lord Dudley (who can be seen in the car). Note the bomb blast wall, which gave a degree of protection to what was an important building.

The great thing in the midst of war is to try and achieve a degree of normality. This little group of drinkers at the White Hart, Aston Road, manage to do just that. The pub itself had previously been damaged by an aircraft coming in low to machine-gun a fire at the nearby premises of J. C. Bell & Co. Ltd.

The Home Guard parade through Rubery.

Officers of the 40th Warks. (Birmingham) Bn., Home Guard, 10th May.

FAT MEN MUST GO WITHOUT CLOTHES!

By A STAFF REPORTER

Teddy Brown.

FAT men are having a lean time now. And entertainers are not amused.

Their trouble is that, in the clothes rationing scheme—and particularly in the new restrictions that are being imposed—the Board of Trade did not take their special needs into account.

When you get fat men and entertainers combined the position in so much the worse.

Teddy Brown, 20-stone xylophonist, is the classic example of such a combination.

He requires six yards of cloth for a suit—he's 74 inches round the waist!—and we 11-stoners a mere 3¼ yards of cloth. He goes to his tailor for a suit for 26 coupons, but is politely told he can't have one.

It would take too much cloth for the value of the coupons.

You can' appreciate the tailor's point of view. For the cloth he'd need for Teddy Brown's suit he could make two for you or me.

But it's a serious matter for Teddy. "I just can't get a suit," he told me. And that's not all. In his profession (he's appearing in "Gangway" at the Palladium at the moment) he has another problem.

ENTERTAINS FORCES

"I must have dress shirts for the show," he said, "but no maker will take an order from me of less than a dozen. I use two each evening; that's twelve a week and there's another 12 in the laundry.

17.5.42

Comedian Tommy Handley. Mrs Mop, played by Dorothy Summers, was just one of the characters that peopled his popular radio programme "ITMA" ("It's That Man Again").

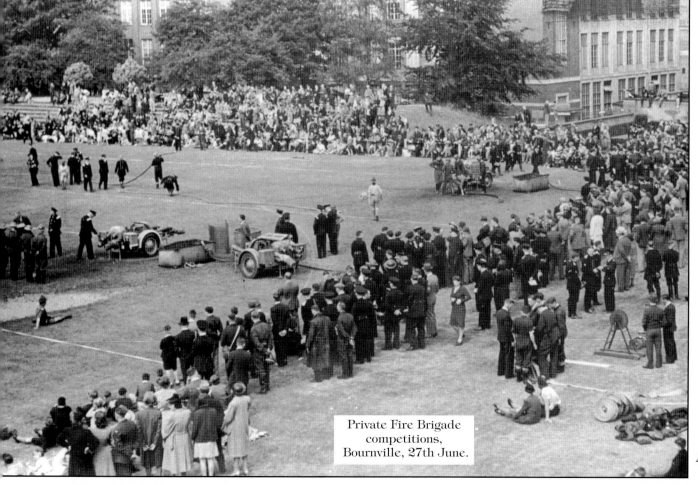

Private Fire Brigade competitions, Bournville, 27th June.

A lecture on rocket projection for Home Guard personnel, 7th July.

Assembling 30-round Bren gun magazines, Austin Motor Co.

eanor Roosevelt, the American President's wife, arrives to see a display of flying (led by Chief Test Pilot, Alex Henshaw) Castle Bromwich Aeroplane Factory, 7th November.

Ammunition box pressings being loaded on to an enamelling stove.

Round-the-clock Stirling bomber production, at Longbridge, means a constant supply of one of the RAF's most successful planes.

Stratton & Co. Ltd., involved in assembling radio receivers and transmitters for the use of the armed forces, West Heath Lido, Alvechurch Road, (known locally as "The Bath Tub"). Stratton, prior to war, was considered to be the leading maker of ladies' powder compacts, pill boxes, etc. They still lead the field to this day.

Bomb primer assembly, Jarret, Rainsford & Laughton Ltd., Stanley Works, Essex Street.

"Really the speedy and final triumph in this war depends not only upon the Government, but upon every manager, scientist, and worker in every workshop, building dock, transport concern and laboratory in the country."

Ernest Bevin.

The United Nations have opened their Second Front. It stretches from Egypt to the Atlantic—2,200 miles—and it is only a beginning. American Forces, supported by the Royal Navy and the RAF, have, says Washington, landed in Algeria and French Morocco—both on the Mediterranean and Atlantic coasts.

According to Vichy attacks in the Mediterranean have been made at Algiers, Oran, Arzeu, and at Cape Figalo, Segalo and Feala, west of Oran. On the Atlantic coast Vichy reports that a revolt has broken out at Casablanca, that U.S. attacks have been made on Fidalah and Safi (the latter 125 miles south of Casablanca), and a Commando raid on Mehedia.

9.11.42

'BIG MONEY' MEN ARE VANISHING

SIR KINGSLEY WOOD, Chancellor of the Exchequer, in a written Parliamentary reply yesterday, revealed that the number of people with incomes of more than £6,000 a year, after deducting income tax and surtax, has fallen from 7,000 in 1938-39 to 80 in 1941-42.

Starting with incomes of £1,000 and over he gave the following figures :—

Income exceeding £1,000 and not exceeding £2,000—115,000 in 1938-39 and 105,000 in 1941-42.

Exceeding £2,000 but not exceeding £4,000—56,000 in 1938-39 and 30,750 in 1941-42.

Exceeding £4,000 and not exceeding £6,000—12,000 in 1938-39 and 1,170 in 1941-42.

Exceeding £6,000—7,000 in 1938-39 and 80 in 1941-42.

He said people with a gross income of £2,000 were paying £359 net in income tax and surtax in 1938-39 and £776 in 1941-42.

Those with gross incomes of £5,000 were paying £1,536 net in income tax and surtax in 1938-39 and £2,757 in 1941-42.

Thread-Line

A.C.2 S. HAYCOCK, of South Yardley, Birmingham, writes us as follows :—

Pass on a few words to the newly-called-up chaps who have difficulty in keeping their buttons on. Try using a darning needle with a four-strand thread. It's easier, and your trousers do stay put.

There you are, you sew-and-sews !

Christmas decorations brighten up munitions' work, Joseph Lucas Ltd., Great King Street, Hockley.

Christmas at Amal Ltd., a subsidiary of ICI, Witton.

The year began well for the Allies. The Germans were being driven back by the Red Army; German resistance in North Africa was crumbling; all Axis forces in Tunisia were vanquished. "The soft under-belly of Europe" (as Churchill put it) was ripe for attack.

The RAF stepped up its attacks in north-west Europe. The brilliantly-conceived attack on the Ruhr dams by Lancasters of 617 Squadron, led by Wing Commander Guy Gibson, gave lots to cheer about. Some of the heaviest air-raids of the war brought devastation to the Ruhr industrial area and to Hamburg.

On 3rd May, part-time work became compulsory in Britain for all women between the ages of 18 and 45.

The United States Army Air Force was now making daylight raids over Europe, putting into place a design that envisaged raids around the clock, with the RAF flying by night and the Americans by day.

The Italian dictator, Mussolini, was overthrown in July, the island of Sicily was taken on August 17th and the Italian mainland was invaded early in September. Italy surrendered and decided to declare war on her former Axis partner, Germany. We had yet another ally. Peace planning was in the air when Churchill, Roosevelt and Stalin met in Teheran on 28th November.

At home, sport still flourished up to a point. BBC radio sports broadcasts were never announced in advance and the venues for games were always from a ground "somewhere in England". Cinemas and theatres were havens of escapism and warmth where we could spend a few hours in comfort and so forget the war for a while. Should an air-raid warning be given, theatre or cinema managers gave patrons the option of leaving at once or remaining in comparative safety. It was a game of chance either way.

In December, the first Bevin Boys, drawn from young men called up for the Armed Forces, went down the mines. Coal was a vital war commodity.

In Germany, as part of their 'Total War' policy, sweetshops, luxury restaurants and nightclubs were closed. Professional sport was stopped and fashion magazines were banned. Calls were made by the German government for the evacuation of women, children and pensioners from Berlin.

The year ended on a high note. On Boxing Day, after a running sea-battle, the German battle-cruiser 'Scharnhorst', was sunk by our battleship, 'Duke of York', thus ending a constant threat which the German fleet was making to our Arctic convoys to Russia. Churchill wrote to Stalin to advise him of the victory. Stalin replied a few days later, ending with the words: "I shake your hand firmly."

Signal Section, D Co., Harborne, 21st Warks. (Birmingham) Bn., Home Guard.

As the Midland region's tribute to the Red Army, a parade of more than 2,000 representatives of the Forces, home services and workers marched through the central streets of Birmingham ; the salute was taken by the Lord Mayor, Councillor Walter Lewis. The workers' contingent, numbering more than 600, was drawn from every branch of Midland industry, and included units from 65 firms. And it was the British workman in flannel 'bags' and grimy 'mac' who got the biggest hand from crowd-lined streets.

The parade later formed the audience at a demonstration in Central Hall where Mr Hugh Dalton, President of the Board of Trade (representing the Government), was the principal speaker. The Red Army, he said, had saved and was still saving the civilisation of Europe and our hopes for a better world. The superb courage and endurance of our Russian allies were an immortal chapter in the history of mankind. The Anglo-Soviet Treaty was one of the greatest achievements of the British Government. We must be together at the peace and after the peace.

* * *

The Lord Mayor saw in operation for the first time the new N.F.S. "ring main" system of water supplies at Birmingham. The system is a development of the national scheme to supplement the water mains by steel pipelines. Linked with supplementary water schemes which cover the whole of Birmingham, the new system makes it possible to relay water from one end of the city to the other in any direction.

* * *

Last weekend the Lord Mayor danced in the club where he first met the girl who became his wife. It was as Wal Lewis, a rising young Trade Unionist, that he went to Aston Labour Club, Victoria Road, one Saturday night many years ago. The Lord Mayor and Lady Mayoress danced the Valetta together ; their two daughters were with them.

* * *

Sir Stafford Cripps, Minister for Aircraft Production, was a popular visitor to a Midlands aero factory when he called on the workers for a rebirth of the 'Dunkirk spirit'. He told them "the more we give of our best the quicker will be the defeat of the enemy

Give of your best and aid the Allies

and the greater aid we can give our Soviet and American allies."

* * *

Birmingham Central fire station, which before the war had one of the most efficient rescue squads in the country, is the headquarters at which more than 250 firemen from the Birmingham and Coventry districts have been trained in rescue work. The training is under the direction of Column Officer W. Mosedale, a former Birmingham Brigade rescue officer who gained the George Cross for the rescue of trapped persons during the Birmingham blitz.

* * *

13/3/43

After the April 1941 raid the site on the corner of High Street/New Street was used for all manner of displays, held under canvas. Circuses and fairs caused it to be known as The Big Top. 22nd March.

A tremendous gale caused the loss of "The Battle for Freedom" exhibition, 17th April. The Pavilions has now been built on the site at the right of our photograph.

Relatives of Bournville prisoners-of-war, 12th April.

55

Eddystone Radio parts, made in West Heath, waiting to be loaded and shipped to Brazil. It was one of the company's radio transmitters, manufactured in their ballroom, which was used to signal the start of the D-Day landings.

Stirling bomber radial engine assembly in the aero tunnel under Cofton Park.

Birmingham Cricket Festival, organised by "Rusty" Scorer, Warwickshire County Cricket Ground.

"The Golden Voice of Radio",
Anne Shelton.

Tommy 'You lucky people' Trinder.

"The Forces Sweetheart", Vera Lynn.

Birmingham excelled its previous stay-at-home holiday efforts during this Easter. City's traffic chiefs reported that Good Friday was one of the quietest days they remembered and during the rest of the holiday transport services were never swamped.

* * *

Deterred from travelling Birmingham people queued for the cinemas, theatres and dance halls all through the holiday period. And — despite the Budget — some business was done in the pubs... For the first time in three years, except for the special peals allowed last Christmas for the victory in Egypt, Birmingham bells were tolled this Easter. Members of St Martin's Guild of Bellringers, the oldest bellringers' association in the country, rang chimes at both the cathedral and St Martin's Parish church.

One of a team of Land Army girls, Dorothy Bond
(of Carpenters Road, Lozells) seems
happy in her work.

Hundreds of pilots, many of them destined for the Fleet Air Arm, learned to fly at No.14 Elementary Flying Training
School, Elmdon. Virtually all the flying was done in Tiger Moth biplanes. Members of the 48th Pilots' course
pose in their Sidcot one-piece flying suits, next to a Tiger Moth.

Because of the scarcity of stockings, women would often paint their legs but it frequently needed an artistic friend, with a steady hand, to provide the seam!

A BOUT stockings all women think as one. Generally our thoughts are unprintable.

Outwardly trivial, stockings have the deepest psychological significance for us. I can explain this by a down-to-earth comparison. Strip most that life holds dear from a serving man, give him hell, and he will never kick. But take his cigarettes away and you are asking for mutiny.

Reading stockings for cigarettes, that is roughly what has happened to women.

We have had to learn to do without many of our trappings, and gradually they have ceased to be important. We can go without.

But stockings, now, that is a different matter. Stockings bring out the deep, deep feminine in us all. Why, the very act of putting on a pair of gauzy sheers is a beautiful ritual in itself, bestowing immediately the consciousness of frailty and dependence in a world of strong, protective males.

Issued Free to the Fighting Forces

Down Our Street

Bert is on the watch for U boats out on the Atlantic. Under the same stars Mum is on the watch for fire bombs down our street. Dick is in Commandos spraying with his Tommy gun but you should see father on his stirrup pump. Mr. Smith's a warden, Jones is N.F.S. Brown is an authority on decontamination. Robinson is ambulance, marvellous with splints. Mrs. R. is ready with bandages and lints. When the walls are falling and the windows blaze then you see some action down our street. Fire engines roaring — quick the hoses out — under debris crawling to get the stricken out. And where the fight is thickest — look! the canteen van . . . Women cool as cucumbers serving cups of tea ! Goering brought the blitzkrieg to their firesides but he couldn't break 'em: now he never will. Everybody's in it down our street — because everybody knows that everybody's needed — Down our street.

* * * *

But Victory is not here yet. Therefore the word is : Still more service, still more saving. SAVE MORE.

. . . — Save for Victory

Issued by the National Savings Committee

Red Cross inspection, Birmingham University, Summer 1943.

Ground crew member, Eric Reeves (of Marsh Lane, Erdington), uses his head to punctuate the joke, 47th Air School, Queenstown, South Africa. The sign actually goes on to read ".. in this workshop without the permission of the NCO in charge".

Badoglio declares war on Hitler

MARSHAL BADOGLIO, Italian Prime Minister, in a broadcast this afternoon, announced that Italy has declared war on Germany.

13.10.43

The annual inspection of over 2,000 Police personnel, Municipal Car Park (behind the Municipal Bank), Broad Street, 12th September.

George Formby.

Formby is Top Again
In Box Office Poll

GEORGE FORMBY, for the sixth successive year, brought more money to British cinema box offices than any other British star. He tops Cinema Owners' popularity poll:

British-born Greer Garson heads the poll of international stars. Here are the lists:

BRITISH STARS. — 1, George Formby; 2, Leslie Howard; 3, Noel Coward; 4, Eric Portman; 5, Robert Donat; 6, Arthur Lucan; 7, Margaret Lockwood; 8, Anton Walbrook; 9, Arthur Askey; 10, John Mills.

INTERNATIONAL STARS. —1, Greer Garson; 2, Bing Crosby; 3, Abbott and Costello; 4, Bob Hope; 5, Betty Grable; 6, Mickey Rooney; 7, Dorothy Lamour; 8, Bette Davis; 9, Tyrone Power; 10, James Cagney.

Leslie Howard had, in fact, died in a civilian plane, shot down by the Germans over the Bay of Biscay, on 1st June.

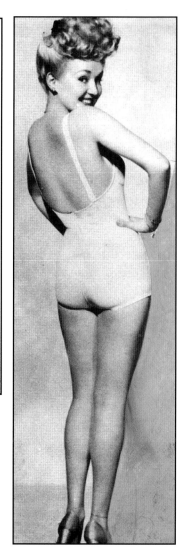

Betty Grable.

In between the films, the staff of the Pavilion cinema put on their own show, Pershore Road, Stirchley. Percy Freedman (centre) was known to the children, at matinees, as Uncle Percy. Over the years, he managed seven cinemas in the city and also worked, as a comic, as Percy Franks.

Could this be the last year of the war? The question was on the lips of everyone. Would we have to endure another winter of shortages? Food, fuel, clothes, beer and tobacco were all limited. Beer and tobacco were never on ration but were always difficult to obtain so the 'under the counter' system applied. Queues formed for most things and it was not uncommon for housewives to join a queue, not even knowing what was being sold.

In March, our military hero, General Montgomery, paid a welcome visit to Birmingham. The year produced a string of successes on all fronts and at sea. Although Birmingham and the Midlands generally did not suffer greatly from enemy bombers at this time, Hitler still had a couple of aces in his hand. However, before he could play these, "Operation Overlord" (the Allied invasion of Europe) began on D-Day, 6th June. Within a week, Hitler's first vengeance weapon, the V-1, was falling on southern England. The launching-sites were pummelled by the RAF and over-run by advancing Allied forces. Less than three months later, from launching-sites deeper into Europe, the Germans relaeased their high-flying V-2 weapons, rockets of vast destruction, impossible to intercept and destroy. The war was still far from won.

On 20th July, a few German generals plotted to kill Hitler. Although the bomb exploded near to him, he was uninjured. Within nine months his fate would be sealed.

In September, Allied airborne troops, many from Midlands regiments, landed near Arnhem in Holland in a brave attempt to capture vital bridges which would aid our advance on Germany and so shorten the war. The bid failed. The battle did not go exactly to plan.

On the Home Front, Birmingham's Fire Guard, numbering some 50,000 volunteers, was stood down in September, to be followed by the "Standing down" of the Home Guard. There would be no more Browning automatic rifles; no more Blacker Bombards; no more sticky bombs and Molotov cocktails. Many Home Guard units had been raised by individual industrial concerns to protect their own premises. The Birmingham Mint, HP Sauce and the Castle Bromwich aircraft factory were some of these. It was only later, in 1967, that the BBC commissioned its

light-hearted series and dubbed it "Dad's Army".

On 15th December, a light plane, carrying the American band leader, Glenn Miller, disappeared on a routine flight from England to France. No trace has ever been found.

The year went out with a bang. German forces counter-attacked in the Ardennes region of Belgium and Luxembourg in an ambitious drive to the port of Antwerp. The battle would continue into 1945.

By the end of the year Birmingham N.F.S. hopes to establish half a-dozen boys' clubs which will cater for 560 Service messengers in the city. The clubs, which are self-contained units, are affiliated to the National Association of Boys' Clubs. There are at present three such clubs and one of them has a membership of 121... A parcel bearing a bright red label "Explosives--not to be shaken or dropped" was brought into a Midland post-office for postage. The senders were informed that the parcel could not be forwarded and expressed great surprise. They said they thought that parcel-post was a quite safe method of transport for explosives!

1.1.44

THE third ballot to select young conscripts for the coalmines was held in Mr. Bevin's room yesterday, earlier than was expected.

Again two numbers were drawn, and the boys whose registration numbers end with either of these two figures will shortly be notified that they are to be directed to do their war work in the coal-fields.

This ballot was held earlier than was expected in order that there shall be no interference with the flow of recruits to the Forces.

It is unlikely that the boys whose fate has been decided by the luck of yesterday's draw will be directed to pit training centres for a week or two.

They cannot be directed until after their 18th birthday, and the training centres are not yet working smoothly enough to absorb them all.

29.1.44

Panel doctors get 9d. more

Panel doctors have been given a war bonus of ninepence for every patient, which means a doctor gets a total of 10s. 6d. for each person on his panel.

In addition there is to be a corresponding increase in the mileage grant paid in rural areas.

The increases, dating from December 1, 1943, were announced by the new Minister of Health, Mr. Henry Willink, at a conference with the Insurance Acts Committee of the British Medical Association. They are based on a recent increase in Civil Service bonus.

EMPLOYERS who refuse, without reasonable cause, to reinstate Service men and women after the war will become liable to fines up to £50 and compensation to their former employees under the terms of a Bill issued by the Government yesterday.

14.1.44

In 2½ minutes *a lovely* Omelette

It's so easy with dried eggs !

Even if you've never made an omelette before, you can make a perfect one by following these simple instructions. Omelettes are easier to make with dried eggs, because the yolks and whites are already blended together.

What's more, made this way they taste simply grand. In fact in a tasting test made recently with dried egg and shell egg omelettes few people could find any difference between them !

To make the omelette, reconstitute two eggs —that is, mix two level tablespoons dried eggs with four tablespoons water. Add half the water first, stir till smooth and quite free from lumps, and beat well.

Melt a little fat—*lard* is better than margarine —in your pan, and let it get hot. When it starts to smoke it's hot enough. Pour in the beaten eggs quickly, and as they cook, lift the edges away from the side of the pan with a fork or knife, letting the uncooked eggs run underneath till all is set. It should be slightly browned on the under-side.

Fold over away from the handle of the pan on to a hot plate. Serve immediately—and wait for compliments !

Eggs are a protein food, remember, and take the place of meat. And dried eggs have exactly the same nutritional value as shell eggs. At 1/3d. a packet, an egg costs only 1½d. ! And you get a packet a month per ration book—2 packets for children under 5.

Remember : dried eggs are easy to get, easy to cook, and easy on the purse as well.

EGGS IS EGGS !

ISSUED BY THE MINISTRY OF FOOD, LONDON, W.1 (DE3)

YMCA Services Club,
High Street.

I Smell Bananas

What *do* bananas smell like ? We've practically forgotten. But our Noses will soon recognise them when Peace comes—unless we've got Catarrh. For a stuffed up Nose *can't* smell. And Catarrh ruins the joy of taste too. Treat Catarrh and Colds the *quick* way—with ' Mentholatum.' Just put a little of this breathable balm inside each nostril. As you breathe, cooling antiseptic vapours are drawn right up through the Nose. Their effect is 3-fold. Swelling in the Nose is reduced. Congested air passages are thus opened. Sore, irritated membranes are soothed. Breathe *your* Catarrh or Cold away the modern ' Mentholatum ' way. For Chest Colds rub on throat and chest. It draws out the inflammation. Get a jar or tin of ' Mentholatum ' Balm from your chemist to-day 1/5. Also in Liquid form. 1/5 (inc. tax).

493 Squadron Air Training Corps "Skyriders" Dance Band, Colmore Road School, Kings Heath.

A very basic, but nevertheless nourishing meal could always be obtained from the British Restaurant, Cambridge Street, January.

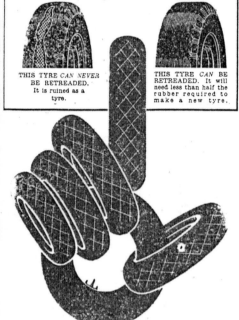

General Montgomery speaking in Montgomery Street, Sparkbrook, 10th March.

Air Training Corps cadets on a training course.

After 1942 a great many football matches were played. In 1943/4 Aston Villa beat Blackpool, over two games, to win The Football League (War) Cup, shown here. Birmingham City F.C. won The Football League South in 1945/6.

Mk IX Spitfires, in the NH serial range, dominate this view of the apron outside the
Castle Bromwich Flight Shed, Spring.

Although Castle Bromwich Aeroplane Factory was known to Brummies as "The Spitfire Factory" it also
turned out 311 Lancaster bombers, some of which are pictured here.

Warks. Home Guard Transport Column, mainly made up of Midland Red Drivers.

The Lord Mayor, Alderman Lionel Alldridge, prepares to open The Lido, Rowheath Playing Fields, 23rd May.

Their newest is their funniest yet! 1,000 laughs packed into 70 minutes of film fun!

STAN LAUREL
OLIVER HARDY
in
Air Raid Wardens

A Metro-Goldwyn-Mayer Picture
with
JACQUELINE WHITE
DONALD MEEK

Plus Outstanding Supporting
Programme including
LATEST OVERSEAS NEWS

AN IMMENSE ARMADA OF "UPWARDS" OF 4,000 SHIPS, WITH SEVERAL THOUSAND SMALLER CRAFT, HAVE CROSSED THE CHANNEL, SUSTAINED BY ABOUT 11,000 FIRST-LINE AIRCRAFT, DISCLOSED THE PREMIER.

Massed airborne landings have been successfully effected behind the German lines, landings on the beaches are proceeding and the fire of shore batteries has been largely quelled.

"Obstacles which the Germans had constructed in the sea have not proved to be as difficult as was apprehended," concluded Mr. Churchill.

6.6.44

THEATRES AND CINEMAS

THEATRE ROYAL, MID. 4-3-5-5
NIGHTLY AT 6.0 P.M.
Matinees Thurs. and Sat. 2.0 p.m.
NOEL COWARD'S
"BLITHE SPIRIT."
FRANKLIN SCOTT
VERONICA ROSE
BARBARA SHOTTER
Fay Middleton Moira Dunbar
Dorothy Richardson
Reginald Atkinson
V Box Office Open 10 a.m.-7 p.m. V

ALEXANDRA THEATRE.
EVENINGS AT 6.30.
Matinees Wed. and Sat., 2.30.
Derek Salberg's Repertory Company.
'FRENCH WITHOUT TEARS'
The Famous Stage and Screen Success, by Terence Rattigan.
June 12th:
"WATCH ON THE RHINE."
Box Office 10—7.

REPERTORY THEATRE.
Sir Barry Jackson presents
"VICEROY SARAH,"
By Norman Ginsbury.
Evenings (except Mondays) 6.0.
Matinees Wed., Thurs., Sat., 2.0.
Box Office 10.30-6.30. No. tel. bkngs.

SHAKESPEARE THEATRE,
STRATFORD-UPON-AVON.
To-night, 7.30: HAMLET.
Wednesday, 2.30: MIDSUMMER NIGHT'S DREAM.
Wednesday, 7.30: KING RICHARD II.
Reserved Seats 3/- to 8/6 can be booked at Dale, Forty's, 83, New-st., Birmingham (Midland 2251); or STRATFORD - UPON - AVON 2271. Please send stamped-addressed envelope for circular.

HIPPODROME MIDland
Hurst Street. 2-5-7-6
5.10 p.m. TWICE DAILY. 7.25 p.m.
"This Way for Laughter!"
ADELAIDE HALL
GEORGIE WOOD
GEORGE MOON AND BURTON BROWN
Eddie, Ready and Joy.
Pepino's Miniature Circus.
Peter Waring. Albert Saveen.
The Three Red Heads.
Len Williams.
V Box Office Open 10 a.m.-8 p.m. V

ASTON HIPPODROME
Box Office Open 10 a.m.-7 p.m
6.0. TWICE BRIGHTLY. 8.0.
ENORMOUS ATTRACTION!!
Harry Benet presents
"FLORODORA,"
With JAY LAURIER,
First-Class Company of Sixty.

PLAYS IN THE PARKS.
CANNON HILL. Mon. June 12.
Basil C. Langton and Company in
"PYGMALION" (Shaw).
Nightly 7.0. Mats. Wed. & Sat. 2.30.
1/6 2/6 3/6 5/-
Booking Kiosk, Victoria Square.

COVENTRY AMUSEMENTS.

HIPPODROME, COVENTRY
THIS WEEK. (Phone 3141.)
NIGHTLY AT 6.0.
Mats. Thurs. and Sat. at 2.30.
Robert Donat presents
ANNA NEAGLE in "EMMA,"
By Jane Austen.
Dramatised by Gordon Glennon.
Next Week. Times as above.
SADLER'S WELLS OPERA CO AND ORCHESTRA.
Over 100 Performers.
June 19th. Lee Ephraim and Emile Littler present
RENE RAY in "CLAUDIA."

DUDLEY AMUSEMENTS.

DUDLEY HIPPODROME.
Phone: Dudley 2-0-1-8-1-1
NIGHTLY AT 7.0 p.m.
Matinees Wed. and Thurs 2.30.
Premier Presentation!
FLORENCE DESMOND
MILTON ROSMER
In a New Dramatic Play,
"DESIRABLE LADY,"

ODEON
New Street,
BIRMINGHAM'S PARAMOUNT THEATRE.
DOORS OPEN 10 O'CLOCK.
A Thrill a Minute in Hitchcock's Powerful Production:
"LIFEBOAT" (A)
With
TALLULAH BANKHEAD, WILLIAM BENDIX, HENRY HULL
Mary Anderson, Heather Angel.
Six Men and Three Women . . . at the mercy of the sea . . . and each other.
Also "GET GOING" (U)
With ROBERT PAIGE, GRACE MACDONALD.
A Thrilling Spy Comedy . . .

GAUMONT
CONTINUOUS FROM 12.15.
HUGE DOUBLE-FEATURE PROGRAMME.
MICHAEL O'SHEA, SUSAN HAYWARD, in
JACK LONDON (A)
Photographed in Sepia.
NORTH-WEST RANGERS (A)
with
JAMES CRAIG
JOHN CARRADINE,
PATRICIA DANE,
WILLIAM LUNDIGAN.
COMING:
THE SULLIVANS (U).

WEST END. MIDland 0-0-2-2
A GAUMONT BRITISH THEATRE
CONTINUOUS FROM 12.30.
Doors Open 12.15.
BEAUTY CONDEMNED TO THE HANGMAN'S NOOSE!
TARZAN'S DESERT MYSTERY (U)
Starring
JOHNNY WEISSMULLER
NANCY KELLY
JOHNNY SHEFFIELD.
Amazing Drama packed with Matchless Tarzan Thrills!
Screened at 12.30, 3.0, 5.30, 8.0.
— ALSO —
Billie BURKE, Donald WOODS in
SO'S YOUR UNCLE (u)
Screened at 1.45, 4.15, 6.45.

SCALA
TO-DAY.
A DOUBLE-FEATURE PROGRAMME.
JACK HOLT
IN
HOLT OF THE SECRET SERVICE (A).
1.57 4.46 7.35
— ALSO —
KENNY BAKER
IN
DOUGHBOYS in IRELAND (U).

FUTURIST THEATRE.
Telephone: Midland 0292.
TO-DAY.
The Plot is Enthralling—
The Music Glorious—
The Players are Outstanding.
IN TECHNICOLOR.
PHANTOM OF THE OPERA (A).

CINEMATOGRAPH EXHIBITORS' ASSOCIATION.

ADELPHI, Hay Mills (A.B.C.). VIC. 1208. Tom Conway, Jean Brooks, in **The Falcon in Danger** (a); Roscoe Karns in **My Son, the Hero** (u). **News.**

ALBION, New Inns, Handsworth 0433. **JOURNEY INTO FEAR** (A), Dolores Del Rio; **CINDERELLA SWINGS IT** (U), Guy Kibbee.

ALHAMBRA, Moseley-road (A.B.C.). VIC. 2826. Tom Conway as **The Falcon in Danger** (a); Margaret Lockwood, Derek Farr, in **Quiet Wedding** (a).

APOLLO, Tyburn-road.—Basil Rathbone in **Sherlock Holmes and the Voice of Terror** (a); **Always a Bridesmaid** (u). Thurs.: Journey Into Fear (a.)

ASTORIA, Aston (A.B.C.). AST. 2384. Robert Young, Dorothy McGuire, in **Claudia** (a); William Tracy, Marjorie Woodworth, in **Yanks Ahoy** (u); **News.**

ATLAS, Stechford. STE. 2208.—Bob Hope and Paulette Goddard in **The Cat and The Canary** (a); Roy Rogers in **Ridin' Down the Canyon** (u).

BEACON, Great Barr (opp. Scott Arms). Robert Taylor, George Murphy, **Bataan** (a), 2.55, 5.25, 7.55. Full Sup. Thurs.: The Falcon in Danger (a).

BEACON, Smethwick (A.B.C.). SME. 1045. Jean Arthur, John Wayne, **A Lady Takes a Chance** (a); Tom Gamble in **Sailors Don't Care** (u). **News.**

BEAUFORT, Washwood Heath. — Randolph Scott, Ella Raines, **The Nelson Touch** (u); **Yanks Ahoy** (u). Sunday: Rings On Her Fingers

BIRCHFIELD, Perry Barr. BIR. 4333. **I Escaped from the Gestapo** (a). Dean Jagger, John Carridine; also East Side Kids, **Ghosts in the Night** (u).

BRISTOL, Bristol-road (A.B.C.). CAL. 1904. In Colour! Betty Grable, Robert Young, **SWEET ROSIE O'GRADY** (U); Richard Dix, **The Kansan** (u).

BROADWAY, Bristol-street. MID. 1761. SABU in **THE DRUM** (U); and **HE HIRED THE BOSS** (U).

CAPITOL, Ward End.—Franchot Tone, Mary Martin and Dick Powell in **TRUE TO LIFE** (A); also **KILLERS OF THE SEA** (U).

CARLTON. SOU. 0861.—SABU in **THE DRUM** (U) (Technicolor); Laurel and Hardy in **A CHUMP AT OXFORD** (U). Thurs.: Falcon In Danger (a).

CASTLE BROMWICH CINEMA. Cont. 2.15.—Eddie Bracken, Betty Hutton in **THE MIRACLE OF MORGAN'S CREEK.** Also Supporting Programme.

CLIFTON, Great Barr.—Tom Kelly and Walter Brennan, **The Adventures of Tom Sawyer** (u) (Tech.) 3.0, 5.50, 8.45. Jimmy Lydon, **Henry Plays Cupid** (u).

CORONET, Small Heath. VIC. 0420. Craig Stevens and Robert Warwick in **SECRET ENEMIES** (A); also **JACARE** (U).

CROWN, Ladywood (A.B.C.). EDG. 1122. George Sanders, Marguerite Chapman, **Appointment in Berlin** (u); Edmund Lowe, **Dangerous Blondes** (a).

DANILO Longbridge. — Lionel Barrymore, Donna Reed, **Crazy to Kill** (A), 3.20, 5.45, 8.35; **Fiesta** (U) (Technicolor), 2.25, 4.50, 7.40.

EDGBASTON, Monument-road (A.B.C.). EDG. 3273. Roy Rogers, Sheila Ryan, in **Song of Texas** (u); Margaret Lockwood, Derek Farr, **Quiet Wedding** (a).

ELITE, Handsworth.—Diana Barrymore and Robert Paige in **FIRED WIFE** (A). Also **THE STRANGE DEATH OF ADOLPH HITLER** (A).

EMPIRE, Smethwick. SME. 0757.—Elsie & Doris Waters, Ernesb Butcher, **IT'S IN THE BAG** (U); Bob Steele in **BRAND OF THE OUTLAWS** (U).

EMPRESS, Sutton (A.B.C.). SUT. 2363. Colour! Roddy McDowall, Donald Crisp, **Lassie, Come Home** (u); Eddie Quillan, **Here Comes Kelly** (u); **Gaumont News.**

ERA CINEMA, Bordesley Green.—MERLE OBERON in **FIRST COMES COURAGE** (A); BILL ELLIOTT in **ROGUES' GALLERY** (U).

GAIETY, Coleshill-street (A.B.C.). CEN. 6649. Otto Kruger, Elissa Landi, in **Corregidor** (a); James Dunn, Florence Rice, in **The Ghost and the Guest** (a).

GRAND, Alum Rock-road, Saltley.—**CASE OF THE FRIGHTENED LADY** (A); **RIDIN' DOWN THE CANYON** (U). Thursday: Now, Voyager (a).

GRAND, Soho-road, Handsworth.—**CONEY ISLAND** (U), Technicolor. BETTY GRABLE, GEORGE MONTGOMERY. And FULL SUPPORT.

GRANGE, Small Heath.—Clive Brook, Morland Graham, in **THE SHIPBUILDERS** (A); George Houston in **Wallaby Jim of the Islands** (u).

GROVE CINEMA, Dudley-road, SME. 0343. VIVIEN LEIGH and ROBERT TAYLOR in **WATERLOO BRIDGE.** Screened at 3.5, 5.32, 7.59.

IMPERIAL, Moseley-road (A.B.C.). CAL. 2283. Don Ameche, Frances Dee, and Harry Carey, **Happy Land** (u); Emlyn Williams, **You Will Remember** (u).

KING'S NORTON. KIN. 1079.—Preston Foster, **GUADALCANAL DIARY** (A); **Man Who Broke Bank at Monte Carlo** (u). Thursday: Waterloo Bridge (a).

KINGSTON, Small Heath. VIC. 2639. Alice Faye and Carmen Miranda in **THE GIRLS HE LEFT BEHIND** (U). Sunday: A Gentleman at Heart (u).

KINGSWAY, HIG. 1352.—Abbott and Costello, **Ride 'Em, Cowboy** (u); also Joan Bennett, Douglas Fairbanks, Junr., **Green Hell** (a).

LUXOR — TIM HOLT, BONITA GRANVILLE in **HITLER'S CHILDREN** (A); Roy Rogers in **King of the Cowboys.** Thurs.: Mister Big.

LYRIC.—Mickey Rooney, Judy Garland in **GIRL CRAZY** (U); also **MRS. LADYBUG** (U). Thursday: Sweet Rosie O'Grady (u) (Technicolor).

MAJESTIC, Smethwick.—Janet Gaynor, Douglas Fairbanks, Junr., Paulette Goddard in **The Young in Heart** (u); also **Fighting Sea Monsters** (u).

MAYFAIR, Perry Common.—Joe E. Brown in **CHATTERBOX** (U); and **MANTRAP** (U). Thursday: Two Senoritas (u).

MAYPOLE, King's Heath.—Preston Foster, Lloyd Nolan in **Guadalcanal Diary** (a); R. Colman, **The Man Who Broke the Bank at Monte Carlo** (u).

NORTHFIELD CINEMA — Frank Morgan, **STRANGER IN TOWN** (U); Rose Hobart, **I'LL SELL MY LIFE** (A). Thursday: Girl Crazy (u).

OAK, Selly Oak (A.B.C.). SEL. 0139 Luise Rainer, Paul Lukas, William Bendix, Katina Paxinou, **Hostages** (a); Bing Crosby, **Paris Honeymoon** (a).

ODEON, Kingstanding. SUT. 2551.—**THE MIRACLE OF MORGAN'S CREEK** (A); also **THE CAT AND THE CANARY** (A).

ODEON, Perry Barr. BIR. 4453. Cont. from 2.0.—**JOHNNY VAGABOND** (U); **THERE'S A FUTURE IN IT** (U). Sun.: Pittsburgh (a); Hi, Buddy (u).

ODEON, Shirley. SHI. 1183. Cont. 1.50 10.0.—Bruce Cabot in **SUNDOWN** (A); also **DUDES ARE PRETTY PEOPLE** (U).

ODEON, SUTTON COLDFIELD.—Bruce Cabot, Gene Tierney, George Sanders in **SUNDOWN** (A). Thursday: James Cagney in Johnny Vagabond.

ODEON, WARLEY.—Gene Tierney and George Sanders in **SUNDOWN** (A), 3.5, 5.40, 8.20. FULL SUPPORTING PROGRAMME.

OLTON CINEMA.—Betty Hutton, Eddy Bracken, in **MIRACLE OF MORGAN'S CREEK** (A). Also **STARLIGHT SERENADE** (U).

ORIENT, Aston (A.B.C.). NOR. 1615. All Critics Agree! "World's Greatest Musical!" IRVING BERLIN'S **THIS IS THE ARMY** (U), in Technicolor!

PALACE, Erdington (A.B.C.). ERD. 1623. Arthur Lucan, Kitty McShane, **Old Mother Riley Overseas** (u); Clive Brook, **Action for Slander** (a). **News.**

PALLADIUM, Hockley (A.B.C.). NOR. 0380. Merle Oberon, Laurence Olivier, David Niven, **Wuthering Heights** (a); Marsha Hunt in **The Long Shot** (u).

PAVILION, Stirchley (A.B.C.). KIN. 1241. In Technicolor! Geo. Murphy, Joan Leslie, 350 All-Soldier Stars, Irving Berlin's **This is the Army** (u).

PAVILION, Wylde Green (A.B.C.). ERD. 0224. In Glorious Colour! Roddy McDowall, Donald Crisp, and beautiful **Lassie in Lassie, Come Home** (u), etc.

PICCADILLY, Sparkbrook (A.B.C.). Vic. 1688. Merle Oberon, George Sanders, Laird Cregar, **THE LODGER** (A); **Schweik's New Adventures** (u). **News.**

PLAZA, Stockland Green. ERD. 1048. Richard Quine and Noah Beery, junr., in **TEXAS TO TOKIO** (U). Thursday: ISLE OF FORGOTTEN SINS (A).

PRINCES, Smethwick. SME. 0221.—ERROL FLYNN in **CHARGE OF THE LIFE BRIGADE** (U).

REGAL, Handsworth (A.B.C.). NOR. 1801. Irving Berlin's Wonder Show in Technicolor! **THIS IS THE ARMY** (U), with Geo. Murphy, Joan Leslie.

RIALTO, Hall Green. SPR. 1270.—**CRAZY HOUSE** (U), Olsen & Johnson; **YOU'RE A LUCKY FELLOW, MR. SMITH** (U), Allan Jones.

RINK, Smethwick. Cont. 2—10. SME. 0950. George Formby in **BELL BOTTOM GEORGE** (U); Nan Wynn in **IS EVERYBODY HAPPY?** (U).

RITZ, Bordesley Green E. (A.B.C.). VIC. 1070. Tom Conway, Jean Brooks, **The Falcon in Danger** (a); Roscoe Karns, Patsy Kelly, **My Son, the Hero** (u).

ROBIN HOOD, Hall Green (A.B.C.). Spr. 2371. Roddy McDowall, Donald Crisp, **Lassie, Come Home** (u). In Colour! **The Adventures of a Rookie** (u).

ROCK CINEMA, Alum Rock.—Frances Dee in **HAPPY LAND** (U); Frank Morgan in **A STRANGER IN TOWN** (U). Thursday: The Rains Came (a).

ROYALTY, Harborne (A.B.C.). HAR. 1619. Roy Rogers, Sheila Ryan, in **Song of Texas** (u); Margaret Lockwood, Derek Farr, **Quiet Wedding** (a).

RUBERY. Phone 193.—Bing Crosby, Bob Hope, Dorothy Lamour, in **Road to Zanzibar** (u); **Sport at the Local** (u). Thurs: The Demi-Paradise (u).

SHELDON CINEMA, SHE. 2158.—ANN SHERIDAN, RICHARD CARLSON, in **WINTER CARNIVAL** (U). Also **CODE OF THE FEARLESS** (U).

SOLIHULL (SOL. 0398).—GINGER ROGERS and DAVID NIVEN in **BACHELOR MOTHER** (A). Thursday: TOP MAN (U); GOLDEN HOUR.

STAR CINEMA.—**LOST HORIZON** (U) (by request), RONALD COLMAN, H. B. WARNER, FULL SUPPORT.

TIVOLI PLAYHOUSE, Coventry-road.—Bing Crosby, Bob Hope, and Dorothy Lamour, **ROAD TO SINGAPORE** (U); Gordon Harker in **SALOON BAR** (A).

TUDOR, King's Heath (A.B.C.). HIG 1161. Margo, Tom Neal, J. Carroll Naish, in **Behind the Rising Sun** (a); Barry Lupino, **Garrison Follies** (u).

VICTORIA. EAS. 0479.—**THE FOUR FEATHERS** (A), Ralph Richardson; **Gals Incorporated** (u), Leon Errol. Thursday: **Flesh and Fantasy.**

VILLA CROSS (G.B.). NOR. 0607.—Carole Lombard, **NOTHING SACRED** (A); also **FARMYARD FOLLIES** (U). Thursday: Texas To Tokyo (u).

WARWICK CINEMA, Acock's Green.—Michele Morgan in **Two Tickets To London** (u); **Follow the Band** (u). Thursday: Thank Your Lucky Stars.

WEOLEY, WEOLEY CASTLE.—**COMMANDOS STRIKE AT DAWN** (A). PAUL MUNI and ANNA LEE.

WINDSOR, Smethwick. BEA. 2244.—Eddie Cantor, Humphrey Bogart in **Thank Your Lucky Stars** (u). Full Sup. Prog. Sun.: Tom, Dick & Harry.

WINSON GREEN. NOR. 1790.—**THE DESTROYER** (U), EDWARD G. ROBINSON. Thursday: CRAZY TO KILL (A).

WEST BROMWICH CINEMAS

CLIFTON, Stone Cross. STO. 2141.—**New Moon** (u), Jeanette MacDonald, 2.54, 4.50, 8.13; also **Hitler's Madman** (a), Pat. Morison, 1.30, 6.49.

IMPERIAL, West Bromwich, WES. 0192. Orson Welles, Joan Fontaine in **JANE EYRE** (a); also FULL SUPPORTING PROGRAMME.

PALACE CINEMA. WES. 0358.—Randolph Scott in **NELSON TOUCH** (U), with Andy Devine, Noah Beery, Junr.; also **Get Going** (u).

PLAZA, West Bromwich. WES. 0030.—Desert Rats & Doughboys in **Tunisian Victory**; also Tim McCoy, Susanna Kaaren, **Phantom Ranger.**

QUEEN'S CINEMA. WES. 0351.—Clive Brook, Morland Graham, **BRIDES OF THE SEA (The Shipbuilders).** Also **JUNGLE SCRAP BOOK.**

ST. GEORGE'S CINEMA. Phone 0737. Charles Laughton and Donna Reed in **THE MAN FROM DOWN UNDER.** Also **IT MAY HAPPEN TO YOU.**

TOWER (A.B.C.). WES. 1210.—James Mason, Carla Lehmann, **Candlelight in Algeria** (u); Sidney Toler, **Charlie Chan in the Secret Service** (u).

'Science-Commandos' Land before D-Day

IT was revealed last night that "scientist-commandos" were landed on the Normandy beaches months before D-Day in order to bring back samples of the soil and sand.

Knowledge of the composition of the soil was necessary for completing the obstruction clearing plan.

"They crawled half a mile on their bellies on the beach with special instruments, taking samples and recording their position, then brought the results back to England," said a civilian expert who had a hand in it and who later landed with the assault forces.

Heavy panzer attacks smashed

THE ALLIED ARMIES IN NORMANDY ARE ADVANCING ALONG THE WHOLE OF THE BEACHHEADS. FIERCE AND HARD FIGHTING CONTINUES EVERYWHERE. IT IS STILL HEAVIEST IN THE CAEN AREA, AND HERE THE NAZI OPPOSITION IS STRONG, IT WAS STATED LAST NIGHT AT SUPREME HEADQUARTERS, ALLIED EXPEDITIONARY FORCE.

In the west, towards the Cherbourg Peninsula, progress also has been made. Our advanced patrols are now west of the main road from Volognes to Mere Eglise. At Carentan—one of the focal points still in German hands—fighting also is very heavy. Trevieres, a town halfway between Bayeux and Isigny, was captured by American troops. The taking of Isigny by the Americans was announced earlier yesterday in the official communiqué.

General Montgomery is in France. He has set up his Adance Headquarters in the assault area, it was revealed last night.

11.6.44

Personal Message from the Army Commander

You have won great victories. To advance 220 miles from Cassino to Florence in three months is a notable achievement in the Eighth Army's history. — To each one of you in the Eighth Army and in the Desert Air Force, my grateful thanks.

Now we begin the last lap. Swiftly and secretly, once again, we have moved right across Italy an Army of immense strength and striking power — to break the Gothic Line.

Victory in the coming battles means the beginning of the end for the German Armies in Italy.

Let every man do his utmost, and again success will be ours.

Good luck to you all

Oliver Leese.

Lieut.-General.

Tac H.Q.,
Eighth Army, Italy.
August, 1944.

General Montgomery, in an unusually buoyant mood, carries out a Home Guard inspection. Victoria Square, quite logically, had long been the favourite marshalling point for parades and gatherings in the city.

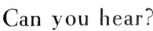

A Co., 8th Bn., Royal Warks. Regt.

The hated blackout finally comes to an end and, as the lights go on, Birmingham celebrates, Victoria Square, 17th September. It was replaced by a "dim-out" which was a partial blackout.

Third from left, Company Sergeant Major Sid Ball (of Erdington) 295 Field Co., Royal Engineers, supervises the construction of a Bailey bridge. The original bridge, along the Autobahn, on the route from Hamburg to the Ruhr, had been damaged by the opposing forces. In the centre crouches a German civilian photographer, working on behalf of the British Army.

Here is the news for which the country has been waiting . . . how the men and women will be demobbed, what will happen to the men now deferred, the new rates of pay for the Services.   Main points are:

After the ending of the war with Germany and while that with Japan continues, young men now deferred will be called up and also men reaching military age, while at the same time demobilisation will begin.

Men and women from the Forces will replace those called up so that there will be no loss of output.

Demobilisation priority will be based on age and length of service. (See Key Chart on Back Page.) Neither overseas service, marriage, size of family, nor having a job waiting will count.

Certain skilled men will be released out of their turn to assist in restarting industry and building houses. They will not be allowed to go back to their old jobs but will work where directed.

No man will be forced to leave the Forces out of his turn and all will be able to volunteer for further Army service. Those leaving out of their turn will lose certain benefits.

Service pay rates are increased as from September 3 by 1s. for the first three years of service for privates with 6d. for each succeeding year up to five. N.C.O.s and officers receive proportionate increases.

Japanese campaign pay will range from 1s. a day increase for a private to 11s. for senior officers. This also applies to troops in India and naval men serving ashore.

The cost of these increases will be £100,000,000 a year.

22.9.44

Peace–by Hitler

From a proclamation issued by Hitler last night:—

Whereas the enemy believes that he can get ready for the last knock-out blow, we on our part are resolved to carry out a large-scale mobilisation of our people.

We must, and we shall, succeed, as we succeeded in the years 1939-1941, relying solely on our own strength not only in breaking the enemy's determination to destroy us, but also in driving the hostile forces back again and keeping them clear of the German Reich until a peace is guaranteed which safeguards the future of Germany, her allies and, thereby, Europe.

19.10.44

H.G.s Now Giving Up H.Q. Homes

Home Guard units throughout Britain have been asked to give up requisitioned property as soon as possible.

Territorial Army Associations, requisitioning agents for the Home Guard, are being swamped with applications for the return of private property to owners now that the "Stand Down" is in sight.

Houses involved run into thousands. Big hotels will come under the derequisitioning hammer, too.

Prospective buyers of requisitioned property have complained that, when they arrive to inspect, permission to enter the premises has been refused and the deal held up.

An official gave "The Sunday Chronicle" this explanation last night:

"These buyers have only themselves to blame. If they had taken the trouble to get permits to enter before they arrived—and permits are given in most cases without the slightest trouble—they could have gone ahead.

Boom in Sales

"They must get the seller to apply for permits beforehand or entry will continue to be refused."

House agents are reporting a boom in requisitioned properties which a year ago were almost unsaleable.

There will be no "Take-it-or-Leave-it" settlements for damage. Experts judged the state of the property before it was requisitioned, in some cases over four years ago.

And experts are assessing the subsequent damage. Payment is to be by mutual agreement only.

Said an official: "We aim to give complete satisfaction."

When the war brought a fall in crowds people said: "Football has lost its grip. The habit may never come back."

Grip? I am officially informed that, although the game is eleven weeks away, a £10,000 gate already is assured for the England v. Scotland match at Aston Villa's ground on Feb. 3.   19.11.44

REGIMENT HOME

THE WARWICKSHIRE YEOMANRY

ARRIVAL SCENES IN BIRMINGHAM

A five-ton American truck stood in Queens Drive, New Street Station. From the cab Private Cecil Pickett, from Buffalo, N.Y., leaned languidly and let drop to the roadway a copy of an American magazine.

He had been engrossed in reading until a train from the Eastern Counties pulled in to No. 3 platform. And then Queen's Drive became a different place, as several khaki sun-tanned British soldiers, marked particularly by black berets with a small badge in them, appeared.

Intermixed with the khaki were civilian fathers and mothers, cousins, aunts, sweethearts and wives and others.

"Sal, buddy," called out Private Pickett as a "Mail" reporter passed him, "what's all the hullaballoo?"

"Oh," I countered, and then, as an afterthought, "Oh, these lads are just back from the Middle East. They've been out there for over five years, and now they're home."

"Gee, boy," said Pte. Pickett, jumping down from his cab, "I can feel a heap how they must feel."

I picked up this little scene at New Street Station the other day when a few of the lads of the Warwickshire Yeomanry arrived home. There was not much more than a handful of them; nothing like so many as left Birmingham—by a strange coincidence from the same platform—over five years ago—for where they knew not.

Since then most of them have been fighting away through Syria, Persia, Damascus, Alamein and Italy. Now they wanted to see Birmingham again—the place, as youth, they left with horses and spurs—the place that has been making tanks and Bren carriers and what not to make them mechanised in a foreign land. They were seeing again folks they had not set eyes on for years.

NOVEMBER ATTRACTIONS AT A GLANCE

MONDAY, November 5th. For Three Days
TALLULAH BANKHEAD and ANNE BAXTER in
CZARINA A
Also Larry Parks in SERGEANT MIKE U

THURSDAY, November 8th. For Three Days
PHYLLIS CALVERT, ANNE CRAWFORD and JAMES MASON in
THEY WERE SISTERS
Also INTEREST, CARTOON & LATEST NEWS

MONDAY, November 12th. For Three Days
WARNER BAXTER, INGRID BERGMAN in
ADAM HAD FOUR SONS A
Also Allan Jones in HONEYMOON AHEAD U

THURSDAY, November 15th. For Three Days
DOROTHY McGUIRE and JAMES DUNN in
A TREE GROWS IN BROOKLYN A
Also INTO BATTLE, No. 35

SUNDAYS at the KING'S NORTON CINEMA

SUNDAY, November 11th. For One Day
CLIVE BROOK and ROLAND CULVER in
ON APPROVAL A
Also Robert Paige in
FRONTIER BADMEN U

SUNDAY, November 18th. For One Day
RANDOLPH SCOTT and J. CARROL NAISH in
GUNG HO A
Also Allan Jones in LUCKY DAYS U

SUNDAY, November 25th. For One Day
GEORGE FORMBY and PHYLLIS CALVERT in
LET GEORGE DO IT
Also Basil Rathbone in
THE SPIDER WOMAN A

MONDAY, November 19th. For Three Days
VERONICA LAKE, SONNY TUFTS and EDDIE BRACKEN in
BRING ON THE GIRLS A
In Technicolour.
Also Jane Frazee in SHE'S A SWEETHEART U

THURSDAY, November 22nd. For Three Days
ANNE BAXTER, RALPH BELLAMY in
GUEST IN THE HOUSE
Also CARTOON and LATEST NEWS

MONDAY, November 26th. For Three Days
GEORGE MURPHY, RONALD REAGAN in
THIS IS THE ARMY U
In Technicolour.
Also MEMORIES (Interest) U

THURSDAY, November 29th. For Three Days
ALAN LADD, GAIL RUSSELL in
SALTY O'ROURKE
Also Russell Hayden in
INSIDE INFORMATION U

Owing to war conditions films booked for this Cinema are liable to alteration at short notice.

The stand-down parade of the Home Guard, Victoria Square, 3rd December.

Property of Major E. Turner

40th WARWICKSHIRE (B'HAM.) BATTALION HOME GUARD

"D" COMPANY

OFFICERS' DINNER

at the

Three Horse Shoes Hotel
Sheldon

on

Wednesday, 6th December
1944

FINAL PARADE

Officer Commanding :
MAJOR E. TURNER

Serck Radiators aircraft design office, Colebrook Road, Greet, Christmas. The company designed radiators and oil coolers for Spitfires, Hurricanes, Mosquitoes, Whirlwinds, Lancasters, etc.

Women's Part In The War

WE COULD NOT HAVE WON WITHOUT IT

No better tribute could have been paid to the women of Britain for their part in the war effort than that of the Queen when she thanked them publicly last Boxing Day.

"I believe strongly," her Majesty declared, "that when future generations look back at this most terrible war they will recognise as one of its chief features the degree to which women were actually concerned in it.

74

Western Command Home Guard.

L/Cpl. C. A. Thompson,
Warwick H.G.M.T.cdn.

Your name has been brought to my notice.

I am authorised to signify by the award to you of this Certificate my appreciation of the good service which you have rendered.

I have given instructions that a note of your devotion to duty shall be made on your Record of Service.

Lawson

Lieutenant-General
General Officer Commanding-in-Chief
Western Command.

Date 1 Jan 1945

This was to be a happier year. The Allies crossed the Rhine in March and Cologne was captured within a week.

Gradually the Red Army advanced towards the Allied lines.

Although it was no joke at the time, the cheese ration was reduced on April Fool's Day! The Italian dictator, Mussolini, was killed by his country's own partisans on 28th April, followed two days later by the suicide of Hitler, in Berlin, as the city was being surrounded by Russian troops.

All German armed forces surrendered unconditionally on 4th May. Winston Churchill decreed that the end of the Second World War in Europe would be officially declared at one minute past midnight on Tuesday, 8th May 1945. VE DAY HAD ARRIVED!

Street parties were hastily arranged. Hoarded food seemed to appear from nowhere. Paper hats and streamers, mainly in red, white and blue, added colour and spectacle to otherwise drab streets and war-damaged properties. An acquaintance recounted how she had carefully guarded an unopened package of 36 Caley's chocolate bars for the celebrations in Norland Road, Acocks Green. (The package was said to have "fallen off the back of a lorry".) In the event, the wrappers concealed display dummy bars made of wood! Anyway, they made excellent fire-lighters for a few days when winter came.

In anticipation of servicemen and women returning home, banners of welcome were made up and erected.

Victory against the forces of Japan was achieved by that country's unconditional surrender on 14th August, which saw the end of hostilities in the Second World War.

King George VI broadcast from London and part of his message was: "There is great comfort in the thought that the years of darkness and danger in which the children of our country have grown up are, please God, over for ever".

"It's no picnic out here.

So don't ease up

on those War Savings

back home."

LET'S SAVE AS HARD AS THEY FIGHT

Birmingham soldiers from the South Wales Borderers,
Fort George, Inverness, Scotland.

Junior Lawn Tennis

William Moss, the Birmingham boy winner for the past two years of the junior lawn tennis tournament at Queen's Club, was again successful yesterday.

After beating Martin Hime (Roehampton) in the semi-final 7—5, 6—2, he defeated Bob Thorn (Kent) in the final 3—6 6—3, 6—2. Thorn had previously beaten N. Regensburger (Aberdeen University) 6—1, 6—3.

The girls' singles was won by Janet Morgan, a London P.T. instructress, who defeated Georgina Woodgate (Beckenham) 6—4, 6—3.

The under-18 singles finals were won by A. J. N. Starte (Cambridgeshire) and Joy Gannon (Middlesex).

"Never seen waves forty feet high, old 'un? Well, them I saw was forty feet, I tell you! Things are higher now than they used to be!"

A touring forces mobile entertainment unit comes to Cannon Hill Park and is met by the Lord Mayor, Alderman William Wiggins-Davies and his daughter Joan.

YMCA volunteers, ready to take refreshments to troops in the area.

Staff of Bournville Utilities, a wartime off-shoot of Cadburys, 3rd March. The firm supplied tools and specially manufactured equipment for almost 100 firms.

Archie Lewis, singer with Geraldo's orchestra, entertains a packed Castle Bromwich Aeroplane factory.
The man, holding the script, was the show's compere, Bryan Michie.

...e Red Cross and St. John exhibition ...at New Street Station last week ...pport of the Red Cross Penny-a-Week ...l attracted the record attendance of ...our—11,780 people. The coach is ...a on exhibition for three days from ...rday at Snow Hill Station.

CELEBRATING VICTORY

BIRMINGHAM PROGRAMME ANNOUNCED

"TIME OF THANKFULNESS AND THANKSGIVING"

Tentative plans for celebrating " V " Day in Birmingham were announced by the Lord Mayor on Monday.

In a statement following a meeting of the committee appointed by the General Purposes Committee to consider the question of celebrations the Lord Mayor said : " Upon such a subject there must always be room for many opinions, but it must be realised that an announcement that the enemy has ceased organised resistance in Europe may not necessarily mean that all fighting has ceased ; many men and women in the Services may still be in danger ; our hospitals are filled with war casualties ; many homes are bereaved ; many civilians are without homes of their own as the result of enemy action ; and the duration and intensity of the fighting in the Far East is still unknown.

" For these reasons it is thought that the celebration of victory will be regarded by the majority of people as a matter for thankfulness and thanksgiving rather than for hilarious jubilation ; and I confidently expect that very many citizens will wish to avail themselves of every opportunity to offer thanks at their various places of worship for the delivery of our nation from a cruel and relentless enemy. Accordingly, whilst adopting whatever form of relaxation appeals to us best as individuals, we must not be unmindful of the feelings of others.   20.4.45

VICTORY SIGNAL VERY NEAR

"BIG THREE" CONFER ON JOINT ANNOUNCEMENT

The Danish home service radio stated shortly before 1.30 p.m. to-day : " It has just been announced that the German forces in Norway have capitulated."

Talks are now going on between London, Washington and Moscow to arrange the simultaneous announcement of the end of the war in Europe. The actual hour of the declaration is still uncertain, but it will be very soon.

There was a growing expectation this afternoon that Mr. Churchill will come to the microphone and say that Germany has capitulated on all fronts, writes a Lobby correspondent.

7.5.45

THIS IS VE DAY
Premier Is To Broadcast At 3p.m.:
Two Days' Holiday
→ THE KING SAYS: →
Crushing Victory

Charles Road, Small Heath.

Some of the ladies of Lingard Street take a brief
pause before the VE party begins, 8th May.

York Road, King Heath.

Lingard Street, Nechells.

Low Avenue/Morjon Drive, Great Barr.

Heeley Road, Selly Oak.

Ashdale Grove, Yardley. All the children were given commemorative mugs, filled with sweets and their names painted on the side.

The Lord Mayor and Lady Mayoress, Alderman and Mrs Wiggins-Davies, arrive at the YMCA Services Centre, High Street, during their evening tour of the city.

A bonfire is lit on the site of the first ARP blackout fire test in 1939, Holliday Street.

The illuminated Victory bus waits for night to fall and the opportunity to delight crowds around the city, 9th-15th May.

"In the Mood"

When people are in the mood to celebrate on the grand scale, nothing on earth will stop them, neither official frowns, nor lack of transport nor lack of formal provision. Hence the weakness of the official Birmingham VE-Day plea that "it was not desired to attract people to the City Centre." They came in their thousands, they stayed as long as it pleased them—on both nights—and how they got home was their own affair. They made their own fun, being in the highest of high spirits; but it was rather thin fun, when you come to think about it in the sober light of dawn.

How relatively simple it would have been to instal bands at the Civic Centre and Victoria Square—and even in a floodlit St. Philip's Churchyard, the Provost permitting—and to have had all ready for the great day a pageant and procession, a sort of free and easy Lord Mayor's Show, behind which the citizens could have fallen in and walked—or danced — round the town. Imagination is what we sometimes lack in Birmingham, and a focus for such great national occasions.

If the "Brum" crowd were not one of the most easy-going and best-natured in the world, so great a concourse could not have assembled at a loose end in a confined space without trouble ensuing. It is a matter for civic self-congratulation that nothing worse happened than the displacement of a few Belisha beacons, and the crowning of Queen Victoria with a trilby, King Edward with a fez, and our revered townsman, Sir Josiah Mason, with a bin-lid.

Hearth-Glow

The real feature of the local celebration, one which reflected the domestic heart of Birmingham, was the way families joined forces in Drab Street and Suburbia and sat down at communal tables al fresco for feasts of surprising opulence and entertainments of all the local talents. Anyone was welcome—a Birmingham schoolteacher who went walking round Ladywood gladly availed herself of warm-hearted invitations to join one hospitable board, and she ended up by dancing a fox-trot with a light-hearted policeman.

The love of a bonfire, so traditionally English, probably burns more brightly in Birmingham than in most places; they ringed the town and lighted the happy revels in places where street lighting was still absent. In suburban sunshine an observer watched a team of almost exhausted boys dragging by ropes the last and biggest consignment of logs to the local bonfire. One poor chappie gave out, whereupon the Boss Ganger (Victory notwithstanding) thundered out: "If that log doesn't go on the fire, you do!" The log went on.

An Evacuee's Thanks

Sir,—I am just an evacuee mother with five children. I have been staying here since last August and now it is safe for us to return home, may I, through your paper, say "Thank you" to all those who have been kind and friendly to us, to make our stay a very happy one.

I would also like to say "Thanks" to the teachers. I am very pleased with the education my children have received in the Council schools here. May God bless you all, and good luck Birmingham.—Yours, etc.,

R. E. READ.

Birmingham 15.

The Union Jack

Sir,—Already many Union Jacks are flying upside down, a signal of distress. May I be permitted to remind some of your readers that the broad white part of the diagonal stripe should be uppermost in that part of the Union Jack which is in contact with the pole?—Yours, etc.,

SCOUTMASTER.

From Birmingham suburbs and Midland districts *Evening Despatch* reporters have sent in flashes on how the people reacted to the glad news.

All the suburbs speedily broke into a vivid rash of flags and bunting. And, as ever, the meanest little streets showed themselves possessed of the greatest local pride. Anywhere that a flag could be tied, there one flew. The response was sweeping, joyful, impulsive.

Here and there an illuminated V-sign kept the fast-closing cloak of night at bay. A bonfire or two sent up lurid flames. Fireworks, carefully preserved since the last pre-war Guy Fawkes night, spluttered and seared into the sky.

Old and young came out to dance in the streets.

Effigy of Hitler

Nechells: Highlight of the bunting across the streets was a huge effigy of Hitler.

Weoley Castle: A 30ft. trunk of a tree was sawn up into logs ready for to-night's bonfire.

GERMANY'S UNCONDITIONAL SURRENDER

KING VOICES HIS PEOPLE'S THANKS FOR GREAT DELIVERANCE

PRIME MINISTER'S STIRRING MESSAGE

11.5.45

At three o'clock on Tuesday, Mr. Churchill broadcast the news that the war in Europe was at an end, and at nine o'clock the King spoke over the wireless to his peoples throughout the Empire.

The actual signing of the act of unconditional surrender by Germany to Great Britain, the United States and Russia, took place on Monday morning at 2.41 at General Eisenhower's headquarters and the agreement was ratified and confirmed in Berlin on Tuesday.

Lord Mayor's Appeal for Victory Fund

The Lord Mayor of Birmingham's War Relief Fund has launched a special appeal on behalf of the city's Service men and women. All money subscribed will be devoted exclusively to the rehabilitation into civilian life of Service men and women. His Lordship writes:—

To mark the victory over Germany the Committee of the Lord Mayor of Birmingham's War Relief Fund has decided to make a special appeal on behalf of Birmingham's Service men and women. This appeal is being launched to-day under the title "Services Victory Fund." I ask the citizens of Birmingham to give their most generous support to this Victory Fund.

All money subscribed will be administered by my War Relief Fund but will be devoted exclusively to the rehabilitation into civilian life of the men and women who have served us so gallantly and so faithfully.

I am well aware that no man or woman will be discharged from the Forces without a gratuity, and that other measures have been taken to ease the difficult problem of changing over from war to peace. But there must inevitably be many cases in which a little extra help, if available at the right time, will make all the difference between success or failure, happiness or discontent. The Birmingham must see to it that no genuine request goes unanswered for lack of funds.

£50,000,000 HOUSE BUILDING IN BIRMINGHAM

Speaking to-day at the first of a series of meetings arranged by the Birmingham Association of Building Trades Employers, Mr. H. J. Manzoni, the city surveyor, estimated that there was about £50,000,000 worth of house building work to be done in and about the city in the next 10 to 20 years.

He was referring to the need for the production of about 100,000 houses to get over the shortage.

When Service personnel returned, he said, there would be from 10,000 to 20,000 families either without homes or living with relatives.

NEXT Thursday, there is to be another Midland broadcast of "Strike a Home Note."

Dick Lawlor will be the compere, and those taking part will include the Arden Singers, about whom I have written previously. This is a choir of 16 girls, ranging in age from 16 to 20, and they are justly proud of having given "command performances" before Gen. Devers, of the United States Army, and Gen. de Gaulle, and of having given upwards of 400 concerts in the past four or five years. All the girls live in the Birmingham area and have been working in munition factories.

Also in the programme will be Eveline Stevenson, Birmingham soprano, with a radio experience going back to 1922, and Vernon Adcock and his dance orchestra. Vernon is another seasoned broadcaster — he has made more than 200 solo broadcasts, to say nothing of the occasions when his band has been on the air.

He is essentially a Birmingham musician, for he was born in the city and studied music at the Birmingham and Midland Institute. He began his career in cinema orchestras in the days of the silent pictures.

BIRMINGHAM CHILDREN USED DUSTBIN LIDS TO MAKE THEIR V-PARADE BANDS

Parties had to be seen to be believed

"IN going round the city I have been greatly impressed by the response of the people of Birmingham to the appeal that the V-days should be celebrated soberly-yet with enthusiasm," the Lord Mayor (Ald. W. T. Wiggins-Davies) told an "Evening Despatch" reporter to-day.

"The enthusiasm displayed throughout the city was extraordinary. In all parts it was the same—there were parties in the streets and the provision for those parties had to be seen to be believed.

"So it was with the decorations. The children were amply provided for. It was gratifying to see how well the parents had contrived to make the occasion memorable for the children.

At one place I was asked to present to the children some 60 books of war savings certificates. I was told that the money had been collected for the provision of A.R.P. equipment.

"I was impressed, too, by the way in which the children had contrived to get bands. I don't know whether the children made impressive use of dustbin lids.

"I only hope, now that V-days are over, that the children will be good enough to return the lids to the right bins."

People who decided to spend V-plus-1 Day as a stay at home holiday went, in the afternoon, into the local parks, where special concerts were given.

Then the police interfered, and the mobile bonfire was dragged away. But it came trundling round again.

Belisha beacons in the Square became footballs, everybody was dancing or marching about with arms linked right across the road.

"We won't go home till morning," they sang. And they didn't. Many of the bonfires which had turned night into day were still smouldering yesterday morning.

In some streets there had been fires every hundred yards. Even before the ashes were cleared away new fires were being built.

Then the crowds began to surge into town again. Here and there the brightest among them started jitterbugging in the streets. They soon had audiences which blocked the entire width.

A band in Victoria Square played programmes well spiced with items to start the crowd singing.

Dunkirk conductor

It was from the Austin branch of the British Legion, conductor, Mr. S. Dimsdale, who lost a leg at Dunkirk.

When the band stopped to get its breath amplified gramophone music took up the rhythm.

Night came again, but the crowds were not those of V-night. There was plenty of fun to be got nearer home, sports with tarmacadam streets as tracks, for the kiddies, then the bonfires again.

Savings stamp prizes

Mrs. Jarvis, Mrs. Hughes, Mrs. Spencer, and Mrs. Yardley, four soldiers' wives, were the organisers of this affair at the Grove.

Savings stamps were given as prizes for the street races and as presents to the 44 boys and girls who shared in the treat arranged by the parents in the upper half of Cato-street, Duddeston.

Here Mrs. Wilkinson, Mrs. Harris, Mrs. Scrivens, Mrs. Griffiths, Mrs. Booth, Mrs. Horton, Mrs. Davis, Mrs. Campbell, and Mrs. Stanley made the arrangements, which included a 4lb. of sweets per head.

There were 100 children from Glenpark-road, Washwood Heath, entertained right royally at Nansen-road school, where Mrs. Marjorie Woods was the leading spirit among the willing parents, who not only worked hard to make the kiddies' event a success, but later followed on with a social and dance on their own.

Sheldon was well to the 'fore with V-party preparations.

Maypoles and fancy dress appeared in Lyndon-road, Dovercourt-road, Rosecroft-road and Barn-lane.

The children of Kingston-road, Small Heath, enjoyed one of the best efforts of the city. Planned by Mrs. Reason and five neighbours, the party excelled, and finally, each child received a toy made by the Wednesday night

inghostel and watching him as he fetched and carried for the party guests was his ninemonths-old daughter whom he had not seen until he got back from captivity.

Thanksgiving Service, Hall of Memory, 9th May.

Thanksgiving Service - and the crowd listens in silence.

Women's Junior Air Corps and Junior Girls Training Corps, Broad Street, 13th May. A Victory Parade attracted well over 100,000 spectators. The Colonnade, seen in the background, has been dismantled and can now be seen forming an integral part of the Peace Garden, in Bath Row.

PACIFIC GAINS

ADVANCE ON OKINAWA IN NEW OFFENSIVE

FOUR MILES DRIVE INTO MINDANAO

Important gains by Allied forces on Pacific fronts are reported to-day. A new offensive has begun on the island of Okinawa, nearest battlefield to Japan 325 miles to the north-east. General MacArthur has struck again in the Philippines.

The latest Okinawa offensive was launched by American forces after they had smashed Japanese concerted air blows

12.5.45

The final toll

The official totals of air raid casualties in Birmingham during the whole period of the war were:

	Men	Women	Children	Total
Killed:	1,172	858	211	2,241
Seriously injured	1,946	846	218	3,010
Slightly injured	2,555	925	202	3,682
Total casualties:				8,933

'The Last of Our Enemies is Laid Low!'

Broadcasting at midnight on August 14, 1945, the Prime Minister said " Japan has today surrendered. The last of our enemies is laid low !" The next two days were proclaimed public holidays, and the spate of rejoicing that had prematurely overflowed in the welter of rumour became like a mighty torrent in the accomplished fact.

AUGUST 15th, 1945

To most of us, even to those enjoying a special holiday, to-day is much like any other day this summer—rather cold for the time of year and disappointingly wet. Housewives are worried as usual over the endless search for varied food, for shoes for the children and for household goods. The youngsters are enjoying a mild excitement, and one fears doing a lot of damage, foraging for materials for bonfires. Life will not become noticeably easier or even different for a long time to come. Yet this date will become fixed in history as one of the turning points in world affairs. It was ushered in at midnight by the announcement in the Allied capitals of Japan's final surrender. In the early hours of the morning a French jury condemned to death the twelfth Marshal of France to incur this sentence. Before noon the King opened a new Parliament elected by the people to carry through a radical programme of change in the organisation of our national life. Though all these events have roots in the past and will condition the future for generations, their coincidence to-day is irresistibly dramatic.

Japan's surrender, coming so soon after Germany's and accelerated by the atomic bomb, marks the downfall of aggressive Imperialism. It has happened before to would-be world conquerors and mankind has hailed the event as the end of war itself. To-day we are less confident than some of our forefathers.

THE SHOW WENT ON

DURING the past five years the bombs dropped in Aston. Houses were battered to dust, people were killed. But they carried on.

And the stage, which began in the church, carried on also. So, last night, the man whose surplice was seen in the door, hard days in bomb-battered Aston, came on to the stage of Aston Hippodrome and said "Thank you" to the stage.

He was Father E. Lewis Blood. As vicar of St. Stephen's Newtown-row, it fell to him to succour many a victim of the blitz. As chaplain of the stage he came on between the acts to say "Thank you" to the troupers who had carried on.

He thanked them for their twice-nightly shows, for the entertainment they had brought to those whose nerves and homes were torn by the blitz.

And, having said "Thank you," he went off—and the show went on.

Military Medal has been awarded to Sergeant Reuben Houghton, Royal Artillery, of Birmingham, for services in North-West Europe.

The citation states: " On the 16 April, 1945, Sgt. Houghton was in charge of a Valentine 17-pounder self-propelled gun. The advance of Fifth Black Watch towards Dotlingen had been held up by an enemy self-propelled gun which was causing casualties and doing a lot of damage in the area occupied by "A" Company.

Crew baled out

Sergeant Houghton went forward with his troop commander to the forward platoon locality from which they were able to locate the enemy gun.

THOUGH the Japanese surrender dated from August 14, 1945, the Emperor' orders for all his forces to cease fire were not issued until August 16. It was anticipated that some delay in these order becoming effective in China, Bougainville New Guinea, the Philippines and other distant areas would be likely, but the Emperor' surrender broadcast made it clear that members of the Imperial family would be sent to some fronts to enforce the orders personally

Fighting continued at a number of points with the Russians advancing rapidly on several fronts in Manchuria (see page 258) and by August 19 they had taken prisoner more than 150,000 troops of the Japanese Kwantung Army, the strength of which was estimated at 500,000. Russian airborne troops by that date had landed in the four chief cities of Manchuria, and at one of these —Harbin—the Kwantung Army Group formally surrendered three days later ; an airborne troops landed in Port Arthur and Dairen (which the Japanese had seized from the Russians in 1905) to begin the disarming of the Japanese garrisons.

IN Manila, 16 surrender envoys arrived on August 19 and were received by General MacArthur's staff officers, to arrange for Allied landings in Japan : these began at Atsugi airfield near Tokyo on August 28 The beaten army in Southern China surrendered on August 22, at Chihkiang, to representative of Marshal Chiang Kai-shek. Formal surrender of 1,000,000 Japanese troops took place on September 9 in the walled city of Nanking, China's ancient capital, and scene of a massacre by the Japanese in 1937.

On August 19 Australian Army H.Q. announced that negotiations, affecting more then 20,000 Japanese in the Bougainville area of the Solomons, and approximately 8,000 around Wewak, in New Guinea, had begun. On September 6 the surrender of a Japanese in the South-West Pacific area (New Guinea, New Britain, and New Ireland) was signed on board H.M.S. Glory (see illus page 327) in St. George's Channel, south west of Rabaul. Officers, ratings and marines on the flight-deck watched Gen. Imamura Japanese C.-in-C. South-West Pacific, hand his sword to Lieut.-Gen. V. A. H. Sturdee commanding the 1st Australian Army (see portrait in page 332). Complete surrender of all Japanese on Bougainville and adjacent islands in the Solomons was signed at Australian H.Q. on September 8.

Quitting of "Tiger of Malaya"

In Borneo, first contacts were not made until September 4. Negotiations for surrender took place at the mouth of the Sarawak River two days later, between Gen. Yamamura and Australian representatives, and formal surrender to Major-Gen. Wootten commanding the Australian 9th Division was made on September 10 at Labuan.

The "Tiger of Malaya," Gen. Yamashita surrendered the battered remnants of Japanese forces at Baguio on Luzon in the Philippines on September 3. Specially brought from Tokyo to witness the ceremony were Gen. Jonathan Wainwright, U.S commander of Corregidor, and Lieut.-Gen A. E. Percival, British commander at Singapore, who had both surrendered to Yamashita when Japan was at the height of her triumph. On the same day, surrenders of the Pacific islands of Truk (Carolines), Palau the Bonins, Pagan and Rota (last remaining Japanese stronghold in the Marianas) were made aboard U.S. warships.

As with VE Day, Victory over Japan was celebrated in much the same way, The Limes, Osborn Road, Sparkbrook, 15th August.

Before the party begins, time for a pause for the camera, Ryland Road, Edgbaston

BONFIRES—IN EXCLUSIVE DWELLING PLACES, AND IN SLUMLAND—TOLD THE TALE OF VICTORY

Birmingham awakened to "dying embers" of non-stop celebration

SMOKE rising from dying embers. Streets littered with paper and broken bottles. — These were the remnants of Birmingham's non-stop midnight to midnight celebration of peace. It was the VJ-day after the VJ (very joyful) night before.

The children of Wood Lane/Grosvenor Road, Harborne.

Victory
England
Russia
America

V FOR Victory, E for England, R for Russia and A for America, spells Vera—the name Mr. and Mrs. Watson, of B188, Dudley-road, Ladywood, Birmingham, have given the Victory baby born at 3.30 a.m. on V-day.

Another V-baby, born while a bonfire was leaping and crackling in the street outside, was the daughter of Mrs. E. Syner of 4/320, Bridge-street, West Hockley.

Democracy of the Streets

How Peace Came to Birmingham

An Englishman has an infinite capacity to enjoy himself, despite what foreigners reiterate about reserved and phlegmatic Britons. Maybe the process of warming up to open friendliness is a slow one, but the spirit is there, even though it be dormant.

It requires occasions like VE-Day and VJ-Day to bring it really to the surface on a grand co-operative basis, and those of our American cousins who are still with us in Birmingham may revise their ideas about stodginess and national shyness after what happened yesterday.

Fun and Frolic

The city had no organised plan of celebrations. The people celebrated victory according to their own desires, and that was why this day-long public expression of joy was so successful and so spontaneous. From early morning thousands roamed up and down the main streets. Thoroughfares like New Street and Corporation Street carried thousands of folks bent on merriment.

It was a colourful picture. The early morning rain gave way to afternoon sunshine, and the folks then really "went to town." Scores came along in fancy dress. There were impromptu concerts and dances in almost every side street, and Victoria Square, of course, was the main target area for Mr. Brum and his large family. At one time there were over 30,000 people milling around, caught in the mad grip of delirious pleasure. The pent-up emotions of six years of war were let loose. "Get it out of your system" seemed to be the general advice, and they did.

It was when darkness fell that the climax came to all this fun and frolic. Where the people got the energy from made one wonder. It was non-stop movement. It was a risky business, as well as tedious, driving a car where the crowds were. It was an automatic invitation to the revellers to climb on the roof or the bonnet, or lay on the mudguard wings. The wise driver used the side streets and made wide detours. The public-houses turned their customers out at 11 o'clock and the crowds grew bigger and bigger, and, of course, more boisterous. It was a much bigger concourse of jollity-makers than celebrated on VE-Day.

Flames and Shadows

The youngsters had their celebrations nearer home. In many a side street there were afternoon tea parties, and after dark leaping flames from thousands of bonfires cast grotesque shadows on the buildings around. It had been an all-day forage for fuel, and it was amazing to see what the folks really did burn —old furniture, mattresses, branches of trees and even garden gates and garage doors!

No finer tribute can be paid to the orderliness of the crowds than was paid by the Birmingham police this morning. "There were no disgraceful scenes and we have nothing to report," was the message passed on to the "Mail." The N.F.S., too, had pretty much the same story to tell—nine turnouts to fires, but no major flare-ups!

A tour of Birmingham's suburbs yesterday afternoon brought once more a revelation of the amazing intensity of the patriotic fervour of the poorer quarters of a great industrial city. Perhaps it is because the inhabitants of Mean Street are less self-conscious than select Suburbia; perhaps it is because life offers so little to those who live under the shadows of factory walls that they let themselves go on such occasions as this. Whatever the reason, it is an almost mathematical rule that the poorer the street the finer the show of flags and bunting; the greater the zest with which the people enter into the rejoicings at the nation's victory.

Youth the Ruler

It will cheer the humanist's heart to notice, too, that in every case it is the children who rule the celebrations. Everything seems to be arranged for the delight of the youngsters. Under a forest of flags, some of which proclaim "God Save the King," you will find some self-appointed father of the street, sweating in his shirt-sleeves while he organises races down the middle of the road or helps to drag a tuneless piano out into the street for the swarming children to dance. Mothers and aunts and grown-up sisters, arms akimbo, take up strategic positions on the doorsteps and watch with indulgent smiles, or busy themselves with preparations for the outdoor tea-party. Whatever it is, it all seems to be for the children.

Down one side street you may find a jovial fellow leading a motley procession in fancy dress making a hideous noise on tin trays, dustbin lids, squeakers and empty boxes. One admires both his indifference to criticism and the selflessness with which he has given up part at least of his holiday to amuse the kiddies. Sometimes one comes upon an unlit or incompleted bonfire perilously near to the buildings.

Sea of Dancers

There is a delightful classlessness about these spontaneous gatherings in the poorer quarters of the city. In one street our car ran into a free-for-all dance. As a "Mail" photographer got out of the car the local humourist bellowed: "Lumme, folks, 'ere's the bloomin' landlord. Where's that brick?" But within a moment the photographer had been swamped by the sea of dancers, and it was some time before he was permitted to emerge and get on with the business for which he had come. Some of the liveliest festivities were found in the most seriously bombed districts but, curiously, the derelict sites were not used for the erection of bonfires or the holding of parties. The ruined houses had been stripped of their last wood—how any of it survived last May is a mystery—but one wondered whether painful or sacred memories still clung to these pathetic scars, to make them unfit places for dancing and festivities. How remote now seem those days when darkness brought the uncertainty of not knowing whether one would ever see another dawn!

All Communications must be addressed to the Department and not to individuals

CITY OF BIRMINGHAM
AIR RAID PRECAUTIONS DEPARTMENT
RUSKIN CHAMBERS
191 CORPORATION STREET
BIRMINGHAM 4

G. D. Read
Air Raid Precautions Officer

Telephone: CENtral 3031

Your reference....................

In your reply please quote...... SHE/H/RS. 2.

BD. 559   13.9.45

Dear Sir/Madam,

I would refer to your recent application for the removal of your shelter, and would inform you that the latest instructions of His Majesty's Government, which have just come to hand, point out that at the present moment neither labour, transport nor storage accommodation is available for the removal of individual shelters, nor is it likely to be available for some considerable time after the cessation of hostilities.

It must be appreciated that all labour, etc. must be used for the provision of housing accommodation for those persons requiring same, and in the meantime, persons having the custody of shelters will remain under an obligation to retain all parts in such a condition as to avoid deterioration, although there is no objection to shelters being dismantled, except in those instances where Anderson Shelters are connected to a drain, in which instance expert advice should be obtained.

The Ministry point out that persons can buy their Anderson Shelters, in situ, for the sum of £1.0.0., or a Morrison Shelter, in situ, for the sum of £1.10.0. Should you desire to purchase your shelter, I shall be pleased if you will forward the appropriate remittance to the above address.

Yours faithfully,

George L. Read.

Acting Air Raid Precautions Officer.

VJ PARADE IN BERLIN

ZHUKOV CALLS FOR ENDURING PEACE

RELEASE FROM FEAR OF AGGRESSION

Marshal Zhukov, conqueror of Berlin, took the salute from the troops of the four Allies in the Tiergarten to-day, in celebration of "the victory of right over the black forces of aggression in the Far East." He called for "an organisation of just, enduring and complete peace."

Berlin's official VJ parade swirled past the scarred battleground in the centre of the capital to a climax of thunderous noise made by more than 50 65-ton Soviet tanks.

These Soviet steel monsters, with guns apparently twice as large as the American 75's, furnished the day's sensation. Virtually no spectator of the three other Allies had seen them before. Soviet junior officers refused to say anything to correspondents about the tanks.

Resplendent in a blue uniform, with three 14-inch rows of medals and decorations on his tunic, Russia's peerless Field Commander in Europe reviewed Allied might.

DUNKIRK MEN FREE

THREE YEARS' ORDEAL IN JAP COPPER MINES

SINGAPORE CAPTIVES ATE SNAILS

At many points in the Far East intensified progress was made to-day with the evacuation of Allied prisoners, including large numbers of British. At Singapore it was expected that all the British survivors of the siege would be on board the rescue ships by this afternoon.

From camps in Japan proper about 8,000 British, Australian, American and Dutch have, it is estimated by Reuter's correspondent at Yokohama, been released up to the present. This represents about one-quarter of the total. Four out of five of all Japan's prisoners are estimated to have survived the treatment they received.

7/9/45

Campaign Stars, Clasps and Medals

instituted in recognition of service in the war of 1939-45

NUMBER OF STARS, MEDALS, CLASPS or EMBLEMS ENCLOSED | 4-1

Order of Wearing		Description of Ribbon	Clasp or Emblem (if awarded)
1	1939-45 Star	Dark blue, red and light blue in three equal vertical stripes. This ribbon is worn with the dark blue stripe furthest from the left shoulder.	Battle of Britain
2	Atlantic Star	Blue, white and sea green shaded and watered. This ribbon is worn with the blue edge furthest from the left shoulder.	Air Crew Europe or France and Germany
3	Air Crew Europe Star	Light blue with black edges and in addition a narrow yellow stripe on either side.	Atlantic or France and Germany
4	Africa Star	Pale buff, with a central vertical red stripe and two narrower stripes, one dark blue, and the other light blue. This ribbon is worn with the dark blue stripe furthest from the left shoulder.	8th Army or 1st Army or North Africa 1942-43
5	Pacific Star	Dark green with red edges, a central yellow stripe, and two narrow stripes, one dark blue and the other light blue. This ribbon is worn with the dark blue stripe furthest from the left shoulder.	Burma
6	Burma Star	Dark blue with a central red stripe and in addition two orange stripes.	Pacific
7	Italy Star	Five vertical stripes of equal width, one in red at either edge and one in green at the centre, the two intervening stripes being in white.	
8	France and Germany Star	Five vertical stripes of equal width, one in blue at either edge and one in red at the centre, the two intervening stripes being in white.	Atlantic
9	Defence Medal	Flame coloured with green edges, upon each of which is a narrow black stripe.	Silver laurel leaves (King's Commendation for brave conduct. Civil)
10	War Medal 1939-45	A narrow central red stripe with a narrow white stripe on either side. A broad red stripe at either edge, and two intervening stripes in blue.	Oak leaf

---

IMPORTANT WAR DATES

1939
SEP 1. Germany invaded Poland
SEP 3. Great Britain and France declared war on Germany; the B.E.F. began to leave for France
DEC 13. Battle of the River Plate

1940
APR 9. Germany invaded Denmark and Norway
MAY 10. Germany invaded the Low Countries
JUNE 3. Evacuation from Dunkirk completed
JUNE 8. British troops evacuated from Norway
JUNE 11. Italy declared war on Great Britain
JUNE 22. France capitulated
JUNE 29. Germans occupied the Channel Isles
AUG 8-OCT 31. German air offensive against Great Britain (Battle of Britain)
OCT 28. Italy invaded Greece
NOV 11-12. Successful attack on the Italian Fleet in Taranto Harbour.
DEC 9-11. Italian invasion of Egypt defeated at the battle of Sidi Barrani

1941
MAR 11. Lease-Lend Bill passed in U.S.A.
MAR 28. Battle of Cape Matapan
APR 6. Germany invaded Greece
APR 12-DEC 9. The Siege of Tobruk
MAY 20. Formal surrender of remnants of Italian Army in Abyssinia
MAY 20-31. Battle of Crete
MAY 27. German battleship *Bismarck* sunk
JUNE 22. Germany invaded Russia
AUG 12. Terms of the Atlantic Charter agreed
NOV 18. British offensive launched in the Western Desert
DEC 7. Japanese attacked Pearl Harbour
DEC 8. Great Britain and United States of America declared war on Japan

1942
FEB 15. Fall of Singapore
APR 16. George Cross awarded to Malta
OCT 23-NOV 4. German-Italian army defeated at El Alamein
NOV 8. British and American forces landed in North Africa

1943
JAN 31. The remnants of the 6th German Army surrendered at Stalingrad
MAY Final victory over the U-Boats in the Atlantic
MAY 13. Axis forces in Tunisia surrendered
JULY 10. Allies invaded Sicily
SEP 3. Allies invaded Italy
SEP 8. Italy capitulated
DEC 26. *Scharnhorst* sunk off North Cape

1944
JAN 22. Allied troops landed at Anzio
JUNE 4. Rome captured
JUNE 6. Allies landed in Normandy
JUNE 13. Flying-bomb (V.1) attack on Britain started
JUNE Defeat of Japanese invasion of India
AUG 25. Paris liberated
SEP 3. Brussels liberated
SEP 8. The first rocket-bomb (V.2) fell on England.
SEP 17-26. The Battle of Arnhem
OCT 20. The Americans re-landed in the Philippines

1945
JAN 17. Warsaw liberated
MAR 20. British recaptured Mandalay
MAR 23. British crossed the Rhine
APR 25. Opening of Conference of United Nations at San Francisco
MAY 2. German forces in Italy surrendered
MAY 3. Rangoon recaptured
MAY 5. All the German forces in Holland, N.W. Germany and Denmark surrendered unconditionally
MAY 9. Unconditional surrender of Germany to the Allies ratified in Berlin
JUNE 10. Australian troops landed in Borneo
AUG 6. First atomic bomb dropped on Hiroshima
AUG 8. Russia declared war on Japan
AUG 9. Second atomic bomb dropped on Nagasaki
AUG 14. The Emperor of Japan broadcast the unconditional surrender of his country
SEP 5. British forces re-entered Singapore

Policewomen take part in the Thanksgiving Parade, 30th September.

The Parade culminated in a Thanksgiving Drumhead Service, Broad Street.

The end of Thanksgiving Week shows that the initial target has been exceeded by nearly £7,000, BSA, Small Heath, 8th October.

Evening Despatch

Gazette Buildings, B'hum.

'Grams:
Evening Despatch. B'ham.

'Phone:
Central 8461 (15 lines).

The Royal visit

THE VISIT OF THE KING AND QUEEN to Birmingham to-day is, in effect, a royal "Thank you" to the citizens for their contribution towards victory.

Whether it be the men—and women—toiling long hours in the factories on the production of munitions of war; whether it be those who, after their daily tasks, have laboured cheerfully and ungrudgingly in various spheres of voluntary endeavour; or whether it be by their savings, the cumulative effect of the zeal, example and dogged determination of the people of the Midland metropolis has been magnificent and overwhelming.

PARLIAMENT has voiced thanks to the nation collectively, in a motion which could not have enumerated the merits or achievements of individual communities.

It is all the more gratifying, therefore, that their Majesties should by their visit single out Birmingham and its people for special thanks.

COMING as it does, at the opening of a new municipal year, the first to dawn after the war, this royal visit should prove an inspiration and a stimulus to the architects and planners of the post-war Birmingham.

There is so much to be done, and so little time to do it in, and the difficulties in the way are so complex, that members of the City Council, leaders of industry, and even the rank and file of the community, may well feel discouraged and baffled.

The Royal procession comes out of Walford Road, Sparkhill and drives along Stratford Road, towards the city centre.

The King inspects the Guard of Honour, Victoria Square.

PROLONGED cheers greeted their Majesties when at noon to-day the King and Queen alighted from the Royal train at New-street station for their first post-war visit to Birmingham when, after a tour of central Birmingham, including a visit to two hospitals, their Majesties went into the Council House for lunch, crowds shouted repeatedly "We want the King!"

7.11.45

Birmingham firms will spend thousands to remove works black-out

BRITISH industry is now facing the first of its big V bills —that for getting rid of the tons of paint used for blacking out glass roofs. It is estimated that the cost will be in the region of £50,000,000. In Birmingham alone the cost will run into hundreds of thousands of pounds. In fact some firms are wondering whether it would not be cheaper to scrap all the old glass and put in new.

14.11.45

" Dad, why is victory always shown as a woman?"
" You'll have to wait until you're married to find that out,"

In War and Peace We Serve

GWR · LMS · LNER · SR

SATURDAY, MAY 18, 1946.

Our Point of View

EMPIRE YOUTH SUNDAY

The British Empire can well be described as a family of nations, whilst our Royal Family can equally well be taken as typifying the best and highest ideals in a happy, united, and useful family life.

Empire Youth Sunday has been increasingly observed throughout the British Commonwealth and Empire since its inception at the Coronation of the King and Queen in 1937. The broadcast services in Westminster Abbey have become a regular feature of the day, and addresses have been given by a young infantry officer (1943), a young Australian pilot officer (1944), and a returned prisoner of war (1945). The following words, spoken by the returned prisoner of war at last year's service. deserve our thoughtful attention. "The British Commonwealth has acted as a family. Its members have shown that there is innate in them that corporate spirit without which no community can live. . . . We have in this great Commonwealth the base upon which we can. if we want to persevere in love and service. build a model for a reconstructed world."

Empire Youth Sunday, which will be observed to-morrow, is in essence a spiritual movement. endeavouring to inculcate in the minds of young people a sense of Christian responsibility towards the great family of which they are a part. It provides a means of establishing a sense of fellowship and communication between the youthful citizens of all parts of the British Commonwealth, and emphasises the need for partnership in shouldering the great tasks ahead. Never, perhaps, in the history of mankind, has the world stood in sorer need of an uplifting, co-ordinating pattern for peace and progress.

THE VERDICT

At long last the Nuremberg verdict has been pronounced. Eighteen of the Nazi leaders have been found guilty. It has been established for all time that crimes against international law are committed by men, not abstract entities—and that such men can be punished by outraged humanity. The guilty include not only those who were Hitler's aiders and abettors, his political lieutenants, such as Goering, Ribbentrop, Rosenberg, Streicher and Seyss-Inquart, but also the soldiers Keitel and Jodl, two Hitler "yes-men" who used the army as an instrument of war, murder and persecution—thus disgracing the honourable profession of arms—and the Admirals Raeder and Doenitz, who organised the unrestricted U-boat piracy and pillage. Then there is Hess, Hitler's closest friend, Neurath, who prostituted the very name of diplomacy, and Kaltenbrunner, who was Himmler's lieutenant and collaborator in all the infamies of the Gestapo — all are guilty men who not only committed the cardinal offence of initiating a war of aggression, but also challenged the basic principles which govern human affairs.

The three acquittals will occasion some surprise, but they only emphasise the fairness of the tribunal's judgment. Schacht may have been the financial genius who made German rearmament possible; Von Papen's chequered career may have held him up to opprobrium and his manœuvres may have resulted in Hitler reaching supreme power; Fritsche may have assisted Goebbels at the infamous Propaganda Ministry. These, however, are not the offences with which they were charged, and the verdict acquits them

1.10.46

Plan for prosperity despite the crisis

AN allocation of 14,000,000 square feet of space in Government-owned factories and licences for 13,000,000 square feet costing £14,000,000 gives the lie to pessimism in Midland industry and holds out the promise of Birmingham maintaining its proud place as the arsenal of the country in peace and war.

These facts given by the Ministry of Supply to the Industrial Correspondents' group shatters the idea that the crisis has roused the spectre of no confidence in Britain's industrial future.

20.3.47

We had won the War; now we had to win the Peace. To this end, The United Nations Charter was signed in San Francisco on 26th June 1945. Could it prove more effective than The League of Nations? "The Cold War", an uneasy peace with Russia, continued for many years and Britain's Armed Forces were maintained at a high level of readiness.

A manufacturing boom in Britain was predicted, but families were still finding it hard to maintain a decent standard of living. In mid-June, Family Allowances were introduced: five shillings (25p) for every child after the first one. Social Security was very much an infant itself.

Demobilisation, based on the maxim 'first in - first out' gathered apace. The demob-suits, shoes and hats were of surprisingly good quality, but the designs left a lot to be desired. Each person discharged received an official Gratuity, credited to a Post Office Savings Account. Though it was not large, many used it to set up a small business and, in the event, became so efficient and profitable that they were absorbed by the multi-nationals. Post-War Credits, a form of deferred repayment of income tax, were a boon to many in low-paid work.

In June of 1946, America was still testing atomic bombs, whilst in Paris, on 1st August, the Peace Conference opened. On 16th October, sentences on the Nazi leaders were carried out at Nuremberg.

The British coal industry was nationalised on 1st January 1947, to be followed in 1948 by the railways and electricity.

The National Health Service was established on 5th July 1948. As though in celebration, bread rationing ended three weeks later but clothes were not off the ration until 15th March 1949. Gas was nationalised on 1st May 1949. The war-time points system of rationing finally ended on 19th May 1950. Petrol followed on 26th May, though soap remained rationed until some threee months later.

Wars began and ended all over the world for a number of years. The United States even exploded a test hydrogen bomb on 1st November 1952.

The horrors of the years between 1939 and 1945 are still being recalled, but, as important events of those war years are being marked by anniversary celebrations, a feeling of great hope for a lasting peace is still paramount.

8th June, 1946

To-DAY, AS WE CELEBRATE VICTORY, I send this personal message to you and all other boys and girls at school. For you have shared in the hardships and dangers of a total war and you have shared no less in the triumph of the Allied Nations.

I know you will always feel proud to belong to a country which was capable of such supreme effort; proud, too, of parents and elder brothers and sisters who by their courage, endurance and enterprise brought victory. May these qualities be yours as you grow up and join in the common effort to establish among the nations of the world unity and peace.

George R.I

HUNTING for an un-exploded bomb with a pneumatic drill may not be just anyone's idea of fun . . . but it happened in Birmingham. True, George and his merry men did not set out with that intention, but when the drill broke through a slab of concrete and almost vanished down a mysterious cavern, they knew what they had found. George, or to give him his full name, Mr. George Colman, 66-year-old Birmingham Public Works department foreman, and his gang of workmen were starting repair work between the Albert-street tram tracks, when they found their "hole."

21.11.47

THEIR WISHES ARE LEGION

EX-ATS, Waafs and Wrens sent a telegram from the Thorp-street H.Q. of the Birmingham Central Branch, British Legion—the only one in Britain with a completely feminine membership — bearing sincere wishes to another war-time A.T.S. girl, and received a reply—from H.R.H. Princess Elizabeth, Duchess of Edinburgh.

21.11.47

WHY SO SHORT?

THE excuse given by cigarette retailers for the shortage — that it is largely caused by the number of men demobbed—appears to me to be strange.

A man cannot be smoking cigarettes in Punjab and Warwickshire, Bremen and Birmingham at the same time. Apart from the fact that many demobbed men cannot afford to smoke so much now, it would appear that liaison between the Services and the tobacco wholesalers must be poor if the supplies normally allocated to NAAFI are not swiftly reallocated to civilians.

F. GARROT.
Hall Green, Birmingham.

'Adolf Hitler is dead'

ADOLF Hilter was officially declared dead on October 25 — 11 years, five months and 25 days after he committed suicide, and his body was burned in the garden of the Berlin Reich Chancellery.

An official notice pinned outside the Berchtesgarden District Court said that proceedings to establish his death had been concluded.

April 30, 1945, was fixed as the date of his death.

On VE Day ten laboratory workers, from James Booth & Co. (1915) Ltd., Argyle Street, arranged to meet up every ten years. Here, Elsie Morris (5th from left) introduces her husband, Howard, to her friends, Hall of Memory, May 1955.

Dedication of Memorial Gate

BARROWS LANE PLAYING FIELDS

In Tribute to the 120 Employees who lost their lives in the Second World War 1939–1945

By the Reverend Charles Crowson, M.A., Vicar of Yardley

Sunday, April 11th, 1954, at 12-30 p.m.

BIRMINGHAM CO-OPERATIVE SOCIETY LIMITED

Looking down the barrels for the last time. HMS Birmingham awaits breaking-up, Inverkeithing, March 1961. The ship gave gallant service throughout the whole of World War Two.

AF recruiting officer, Flight-Lieutenant Bill Clayfield, examines a mb that failed to explode when it fell near the GEC works, Witton, in November 1940. It is to form part of a "Battle of Britain" exhibition, at Castle Bromwich, September 1957.

"Satan", the wartime bomb, used to collect funds for the Lord Mayor's charities, Bull Ring, 13th November 1963.

Herr Werner Nagel (right) and Herr Hans Zimmerman prepare to lay a wreath, at the Hall of Memory, from the survivors of the Bismarck in memory of those who died aboard HMS Hood. 22nd May 1972.

In 1972, Percy Franks, complete with Hitler moustache, recreates a typical pose from his wartime comedy act. During the early part of the conflict, he frequently created hysterical laughter with his impression. By a remarkable coincidence, in "Birmingham at War Vol 1", we referred to the act without actually knowing his identity. It must have been the ultimate in satire, over fifty years ago, for a Jewish comedian to portray Hitler!

The Sunday Mercury organises an excursion to the French Coast, to mark the 40th Anniversary of D-Day, 6th June 1984.

The 40th anniversary of VE Day means a knees-up for the Farnborough Road Residents Association, Castle Vale, 6th May 1985.

More than 100 children turned up for the VE picnic in Sutton Park. Ice cream man, Stan Darby, who runs the park's lido, finds his comic Hitler invokes a suitably comic reaction from some of his audience, 8th May 1985.

are staging an Exhibition

'A City at War: Birmingham 1939-1945'

The Exhibition opens at the Museum on
        Wednesday 8 May 1985.

Alton Douglas, well-known TV and
Radio personality, will be signing copies
of the books he has compiled on
Birmingham during World War II

        'BIRMINGHAM AT WAR Vol. I'
        'BIRMINGHAM AT WAR Vol. II'

in the Museum Shop, City Museum and
Art Gallery, Chamberlain Square,
Birmingham B3 3DH

        between 10.00-12.00 hours
        Wednesday 8 May

Dunkirk veterans, Tom Barnes and Harry Clifton, of Kings Heath and Fred Tidmarsh, of Edgbaston, display their medals before the Thanksgiving Service at Birmingham Cathedral, 8th May 1985.

Instructors at the National Motor Cycle Centre, Small Heath (not to be confused with the Museum at Bickenhill) unearth a cache of wartime helmets, on the site used by the BSA, 14th March 1985.

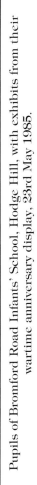

Pupils of Bromford Road Infants' School, Hodge Hill, with exhibits from their wartime anniversary display, 23rd May 1985.

A VE Commemorative Parade and Drumhead Service
is held at Alexander Stadium, 11th May 1985.

Ex-servicemen wait to lay wreaths at a service held to
remember those who died at the hands of the
Japanese. Hall of Memory, 23rd February 1989.

Former members of the Women's Auxiliary Air Force march along Colmore Row, after a memorial service at St. Philip's Cathedral to commemorate the outbreak of the Second World War. 3rd September 1989.

WARTIME W.A.A.F. RE-UNION SERVICE

BIRMINGHAM CATHEDRAL

SUNDAY 3rd SEPTEMBER
1989
2.00 p.m.

Conducted by
The Ven. J. L. Cooper BD., M.Phil.,
Archdeacon of Aston

The Lord Mayor of Birmingham
Councillor Peter J. P. Barwell, M.B.E. Hon. C.S.M.
requests the pleasure of your company at
a Civic Reception to The Warwickshire Yeomanry
in the Banqueting Suite, at the Council House
Victoria Square, Birmingham
on Wednesday 12th May 1993, at 1230 hours

To be presented upon arrival   *Informal*

THE
ROYAL WARWICKSHIRE
REGIMENTAL ASSOCIATION

BIRMINGHAM BRANCH

FOLLOWING the celebrations in Normandy to mark the 50th anniversary of the D-Day landings, veterans of the 2nd and 1/7th Battalions of the Royal Warwickshire Regiment will assemble for an anniversary lunch.

It will be held at the Regimental Museum in St John's House, Warwick, on June 12.

Both Battalions were involved in the long battles for Caen and the subsequent breakout to Falaise.

The 2nd Battalion landed at Lion-sur-Mer on D-Day itself and the 1/7th followed three weeks later.

There will be more than 150 veterans sitting down to lunch to mark the anniversary.

Casualties

DURING the entire Second World War the Royal Warwickshire Regiment had 84 officers and 977 other ranks killed.

ONE name which will inevitably be mentioned with pride at the anniversary celebrations will be that of Field Marshall Viscount Montgomery of Alamein, for the Royal Warwickshire Regiment was Monty's regiment.

From Sandhurst he was gazetted into the Warwickshires on September 19, 1908.

Eight weeks later, on December 12, he joined the First Battalion on the North-West Frontier of India at Peshawar.

He was promoted Lieutenant in April, 1910 and was 26 when he sailed with the Warwicks to France after the outbreak of the First World War.

He was wounded at Ypres by a sniper and promoted to field captain.

By the end of that war he was 30 years old and had reached the rank of temporary Lieutenant Colonel.

Big day

D-Day veterans who missed out on historic 50th anniversary commemorations in France are to be presented with commemorative medals at a special ceremony in Portsmouth tomorrow.

Spitfire sale

A Mark XIX Spitfire from the Battle of Britain Memorial Flight has sold for £452,500 at a Sotheby's auction.

26.11.94

THE French government has honoured more than 300 World War II veterans, war widows and other relatives who were unable to cross the Channel to take part in the D-Day commemorations.

They gathered at Selly Oak Ex-Servicemen's Club in Birmingham yesterday to receive medals awarded by the French.

3.2.95

D-DAY VETERANS
War Widows wish to thank Mr. Fred Crowton for his hard work to get the Liberation Medals here. Well organised. Thank you.

16.2.95

"Here you are, love; I'll make sure he can see the King and Queen",
Waterloo Street/Victoria Square, 7th November 1945.

ACKNOWLEDGEMENTS

(for providing photographs, for encouragement and numerous other favours)

Lt. Commander J.M. Baggs; Sid Ball; The Birmingham Post & Mail Staff; Brewin Books; Ron Butler; Phil Byrne; Cadbury Ltd.; Dave Carpenter; Ron Catton; Central Midlands Co-operative Society Ltd.; Raynor Cohen; John and Jacqueline Coxell; Alan and Brenda Cronshaw; Dave Cross; Christine Davies; Annette Dickers; Eddystone Radio Ltd.; T.W. Ferrers-Walker; Beryl Fletcher; Four Seasons Art Gallery; David Goodyear; Clive Hardy; Violet Hemus; Imperial War Museum; Anne Jennings; Dave, Thelma and Tom Jones; Ken Kelly; Laughton & Sons Ltd.; Sue Letts; Joan Lewis; Ethel Lloyd; Percy McGeoch; Dennis Moore; Geoffrey Negus; Rose Norris; George Peace; Eric and Dorothy Reeves; Mary Robertson; Norman Rogers; The Royal Regt. of Fusiliers, St John's House, Warwick; Jeanette Shanian; Mike and Anne Sheehan; Frank Shorter; Audrey Smallwood; Social History Section, Dept. of Leisure & Community Services, Birmingham City Council; Stanway D.I.Y. Ltd.; Phil Teague; Brian and Jan Thompson; Brenda Treagust; Joan Wanty; West Midlands Police Museum; West Midlands Travel; Bob and Joan Wilkes; Paul and Gill Wood.

Please forgive any possible omissions. Every effort has been made to include all organisations and individuals involved in the book.

BACK COVER: Top left: A soldier waits to direct traffic, from the top of a road barricade.
Bottom: An impression of the size of the production halls at Castle Bromwich is given by
this view, showing Spitfire LF.XVIE's approaching completion, 1945.